T0295519

Gender Equity in Hospitality

Praise for *Gender Equity In Hospitality*

In this much-needed study of the hospitality industry in India, Dr Payal Kumar provides an in-depth analysis of the challenges, as well as solutions, to women's advancement in leadership. Based on thought-provoking data from interviews with senior- and mid-level leaders in this sector, as well as data on gendered leadership representation, this book adds to literature by contextualizing gender diversity and equity issues in India, while providing far-reaching HR solutions needed to catapult the hospitality industry forward.

Diana Bilimoria, Professor and Chair of Organizational Behavior and KeyBank Professor, Case Western Reserve University, USA

This rigorous study on India's hospitality industry from a gendered lens is a notable contribution to the literature on gender and leadership in the Global South. Congratulations are in order to the author Payal Kumar for this invaluable monograph.

Melissa Fisher, Author of *Wall Street Women and Cultural Anthropologist*, NYU Institute for Public Knowledge & School of Professional Studies, USA

Women continue to lag behind men in most measures of employment and income, but the inequities women face in hospitality are even more significant, given greater occupational segregation, unusual work hours, gender bias, work–family conflict, and barriers to leadership roles. The COVID-19 pandemic further contributed to widening the gaps between women and men. Dr Payal Kumar has conducted extensive research and captured the inequities women face in the hospitality industry in India. Her book offers us an insightful account of how a strong paternalistic culture persists in hindering the advancement of women in the Indian hospitality industry.

Eddy Ng, Smith Professor of Equity and Inclusion in Business, Queen's University, Canada

Professor Payal Kumar's book, *Gender Equity in Hospitality: The Case of India*, makes very timely and important contributions. It is a thoughtful book that must be read by every hospitality manager. I was particularly impressed by its coverage of both the pre- and post-COVID-19 pandemic landscape. Practitioners and policy makers will find the in-depth analysis of the barriers to woman leadership in hospitality very helpful. Understanding these roadblocks is critical in helping organizations overcome these challenges. Meaningful change demands a simultaneous focus on both individuals and systems. Professor Kumar's powerful change models are a highlight of the book.

Sukhbir Sandhu, Associate Professor and Executive Director, Centre for Workplace Excellence, UniSA Business, University of South Australia, Australia

The Indian hospitality industry has had a poor track record in regard to gender equality and Dr Payal Kumar's book *Gender Equity in Hospitality: The Case of*

India is a must-read for leaders who want to make a difference. With detailed verbatim comments, it is an insightful read that can help any hospitality company put together a clear roadmap towards achieving its environmental, social, and governance (ESG) goals. I am hopeful that together we can all recalibrate the playing field and see many more women in hospitality board rooms.

Kanika Hasrat, Area Director UP, MP and Uttarakhand and General Manager at Taj Lakefront Bhopal at The Indian Hotel Company Limited, and President of Women Indian Chamber for Commerce and Industry (WICCI) for Hospitality and Tourism, India

Given the importance and pace of growth of the hospitality and tourism sector for the Indian economy, this is a timely study as it addresses the twin cultural issues of a lack of gender diversity and inequitable promotion practices in hospitality and tourism in India. The current undeniable domination of studies focused on Western contexts makes this a valuable contribution to the field.

Ruth Puhr, Head of Quality Assurance and Academic Development, Les Roches Global Hospitality Education, Switzerland

In *Gender Equity in Hospitality: The Case of India*, Prof Payal Kumar draws attention to how cultural nuances and other factors shape and impact careers in the hospitality industry in India. Drawn from extensive research and her own observations, the book contains practical recommendations for policy makers and industry leaders that would enable more women to be included, engaged and have successful stints in the hospitality industry. In a world where purpose and ways of working are being redefined, this is a highly relevant read.

Aarti Kelshikar, Founder, 3A Consulting, and Author of *How Women Work: Fitting In and Standing Out in Asia*

This much-needed book offers valuable insights into the barriers to woman leadership in the Indian hospitality sector, both on the individual and systemic level. It deals incisively with the gendered and gendering problems of the sector constructed at the level of individual identities and cultural expectations embedded into interaction, institutional opportunities, and constraints. This book will be valuable for researchers, practitioners, and policy makers who want to understand barriers to woman leadership in a patriarchal and high-power distance society and who strive for a systemic change in the sector. It will also enrich the lives of hospitality students who want to understand gender discrimination and make a difference in their lives and in the field.

Regine Bendl, Associate Professor, Institute for Gender and Diversity in Organizations, Vienna University of Economics and Business, Austria

Gender Equity in Hospitality: The Case of India

BY

PAYAL KUMAR

Indian School of Hospitality, India

United Kingdom – North America – Japan – India – Malaysia – China

Emerald Publishing Limited
Howard House, Wagon Lane, Bingley BD16 1WA, UK

First edition 2023

British Library Cataloguing in Publication Data
A catalogue record for this book is available from the British Library

ISBN: 978-1-80382-666-0 (Print)
ISBN: 978-1-80382-665-3 (Online)
ISBN: 978-1-80382-667-7 (Epub)

INVESTOR IN PEOPLE

I dedicate this book to my younger sister Leena Khurana,
who has taught me more than she will ever know.

Contents

List of Tables and Figures

Tables

Appendix Tables

Figures

About the Author

Dr **Payal Kumar** is Principal Academic Advisor at Indian School of Hospitality, India, the South Asian Ambassador for *Academy of Management Discoveries Journal,* and Emerald Publisher Brand Ambassador. She completed her Master of Arts from the School of Oriental and African Studies, UK, and PhD from XLRI, India. As a researcher, her accolades include the best symposium for the MED division, Academy of Management Conference, Seattle, USA, 2022 and the Andre Delbecq & Lee Robbins MSR (Academy of Management) Scholarship. She is an Associate Editor for the *Journal of Management, Spirituality and Religion*, and Senior Reviewer for top journals such as *Journal of Organization Behaviour*. She has published 17 books so far, including a 5-volume series on Leadership and Followership (Palgrave Macmillan). In an earlier avatar, she was Vice President of Editorial and Production at SAGE Publications Ltd.

Foreword

Ashish Malik

It is critical that one develops an understanding of the western term 'hospitality' by contextualizing what the phenomenon of hospitality means as per rich and deep-seated Indian cultural beliefs. The notion of serving guests has immense historical, spiritual and cultural importance in the Indian Vedic scriptures, propagated through scriptures and the oral tradition in India. In popular press and wider cultural beliefs, the abridged Sanskrit mantra *Atithidevo Bhava,* which roughly translates to 'treat a Guest as a God' or 'A Guest is akin to God' captures the essence of service, welcoming and invocations that followers of the Hindu and Sanathan Dharam popularly practise. Other interpretations of the Hindu Vedic scriptures of the above Sanskrit Mantra focus on welcoming and serving the 'Brahamana', a person who has deep spiritual knowledge and comes without intimation as your guest. Given this background, if someone turns up uninvited at your place in India, it is common to greet them and serve them food. Many first-time visitors to India return home with stories of the great hospitality they experienced.

In fact, guests are welcomed in a God-like manner with offerings of *Dhupa* (fragrance), *Dipa* (Lamp), *Naidevya* (Food), *Akshata* (Rice) and *Pushpa* (flowers). The Department of Tourism's advertising also captures the *Atithidevo Bhava* ethos and aims to reinforce social awareness through its campaign as its citizens welcome guests into the country. Often women play a key role in welcoming guests.

The promotional campaign and observable cultural practices serve as a good reinforcement and differentiator for the Tourism Department's Incredible India campaign. The campaign helps attract tourists from all around the world, highlighting the differences in experiences of the cultural practices between the West and East, something which was aptly captured many years ago in Rudyard Kipling's composition, *The Ballad of East and West*: 'Oh, East is East and West is West, and never the twain shall meet; Till Earth and Sky stand presently at God's great Judgment Seat' (https://www.kiplingsociety.co.uk/poem/poems_eastwest.htm).

India and the Western world's cultural diversity has been noted in several seminal cultural frameworks, such as those of Hofstede (2001) and House et al. (2007). Recent accounts of India's cultural singularities and social complexity by Laleman et al. (2014) and Malik and Pereira (2016) also further our understanding.

In addition to cultural influences, Indian societal attitudes towards women are also shaped by religious, social and institutional beliefs. India has been characterized as a high power-distance and patriarchal society. Unfortunately, this affects the framing at multiple levels of what should be the professional role of women in India. Despite the promise of rapid growth in the hospitality industry in India, some systemic issues persist. For example, there is still a seeming preference for employing a more significant proportion of men in senior positions relative to women, who are employed more in junior positions (Chaudhary & Gupta, 2010). Among the common prejudices in the industry are that women cannot cope with long and late shifts and can also not maintain a healthy work–life balance (Doherty, 2004). Additional barriers to advancing women's senior leadership roles include developmental discrepancies and cultural discouragement (Patwardhan, Mayya, & Joshi, 2016).

There are several gendered issues relating to the success of women professionals working in the hospitality sector. Building on the cultural, religious and social complexities mentioned above, Professor Payal Kumar builds on her dedicated scholarship that focusses on gender studies in an Indian context and delivers yet another powerful and insightful account of gender equity in hospitality. This monograph is a sequel to her earlier Emerald book on *Gender Equity in the Boardroom: The Case of India* (2020), co-authored with Dr Ganesh Singh. Focussing on a complex range of professional identities and issues of gender-based inequality in Indian society, Professor Kumar picks up on the vital issue of gender and diversity. Such an account is relevant not only to diversity and inclusion scholars but also to critical management studies scholars.

This research is a rich addition to the existing literature, as it bridges our gaps in understanding the differences in the specific role stressors for men and women – including why women experience more significant role stagnation than men. The extant literature does not address this; thus, research on the antecedents for the lack of leadership opportunities for women in India's hospitality and tourism sectors is timely. Researching the state of gender equity in the hospitality industry in the post-pandemic era was preceded by a white paper by the author on the same topic and sponsored by the Women's Indian Chamber of Commerce & Industry (WICCI) and the Indian School of Hospitality.

Professor Kumar employs a two-staged methodology for her exploratory study on this vital topic. First, as a preliminary study, she examines the antecedents of low participation levels of women in leadership positions in the hospitality industry in India. Professor Kumar analysed the data from 23 in-depth interviews of senior- and mid-level leaders, both male and female. These interviews were coded, and then within-case and between-case themes were elicited to understand the barriers to women's leadership. Second, she collected data on the representation of women leaders in three-star to five-star luxury hotels, as currently, there is no such account of consolidated data on this topic.

The book covers the much-debated issues of gender equity or 'fairness of treatment' for women regarding their rights, benefits and opportunities in a society that expects the woman to be the primary caregiver at home. The book also offers comparisons with western trends in hospitality. The findings of this research have important insights for leaders in the hospitality industry. It unpacks the barriers to gender equity at three levels of analyses: at the individual level it was found that women employees face more work–life pressure than their male counterparts; at the group level stereotyping by colleagues and paternalistic attitudes of bosses proves to be hindrance; and at the firm level there was found to be a lack of mentoring opportunities.

There are implications also for HR practitioners, and learners can gain insights from success stories of what HR practitioners did in terms of 'good HR policies' for women, such as including flexitime, which leaders in this industry can emulate. The study findings are likely to be useful as a stepping-stone for policy makers, government and industry leaders to rebound from the pandemic to transform India into one of the top 20 tourist destinations in the world.

The book is timely as the hospitality and tourism industries globally, not just in India, were reeling under pressures imposed by the pandemic and are now on a turbo-charged growth path in the post-pandemic world. The tourism industry is predicted to grow rapidly until the end of 2023, fuelled by the expected expansion of the e-visa scheme by the Government of India. Such rapid growth necessitates addressing several workforce issues such as employee attrition, equitable and fair compensation, and opening up diverse workforce opportunities. These issues are critical as they strongly affect the firm's success and industry growth as an economic driver for the nation.

All in all, this book offers a rich case study account of a contextual understanding of the barriers to leadership that women in India face in light of a patriarchal and high-power distance society. My congratulations to Professor Payal Kumar for such insightful research.

Ashish Malik
Associate Professor
Head of the Management Discipline
Newcastle Business School
University of Newcastle, Australia

Preface

Together with an enthusiastic research team, I began to deep dive into trying to understand the barriers and potential opportunities for women leaders in the hospitality industry. What could be the reasons for so few women making it to top leadership positions in the Indian context? And that too when in other sectors women have done remarkably well in breaking the glass ceiling. For example, India has the highest number of female pilots in the world at 12.4% which is twice the global average, even though this is a profession that involves 100% travelling and also shift work. Financial services and the banking sector is another area where women have stormed the male bastion. In both these examples, women have managed to soar to leadership positions in spite of the gender stereotypes that 'women can't read maps' and that 'women are not good with numbers.' So why is it that women in hospitality can't fly as high, in an industry that one would imagine that women are naturally attuned to?

That this industry is male dominated is pretty much a global phenomenon. Dr Maria Gebbels, senior lecturer in hospitality management at the University of Greenwich, said: 'In comparison to other sectors, the hospitality industry has a long-standing history of being male-dominated, traditional, and paternalistic, resulting in conflicts of power and gender inequality' (https://www.thecaterer.com/news/surrey-greenwich-university-report-gender-equality-hospitality). But I was curious about what were the specific barriers and opportunities for women in the hospitality industry in India?

The results of this study suggest that what perhaps stands out in India at the entry-level as a barrier is the strong stereotype that this is not a suitable industry for women. Long working hours and also the social taboo of women working in bars are distinct entry barriers. One can only conjecture about the 'missing women' – in other words, those that want to join the industry, but who are discouraged from doing so by their family. There is no way to quantify the number of these potential hires. It is worthy to point out that post-liberalization in other industries such as information technology, women have been entering in large droves.

This study also notes that at the mid-management level, many women drop out because juggling the pressures of both family and work becomes too much, thus creating a 'leaky pipeline problem' – where there are not enough female candidates to recommend for more senior positions. And for mid-managers in this industry, upward growth becomes next to impossible unless candidates are up for geographical relocation. I must add that this monograph is not all about doom and gloom, but also about hope! There is one chapter dedicated to stories of exceptional individual success, and also path-breaking gender-friendly initiatives at the firm level.

One recommendation for overcoming the bias of 'think manager, think male' is for industry leaders to reflect on whether a leader necessarily has to be an agentic male, simply because this has been the precedent in the industry so far. They may want to move from this auto-pilot mode, introspect, and rethink the leadership qualities required in the industry, using a different lens, for example, contemplating a style of leadership that may be more androgynous in nature.

This study adds to the literature of the Global South, and in doing so showcases the importance of the national and cultural contextualization of a phenomenon. It is hoped that our pain-staking research on the India story will not only provide conceptual richness to the study on gender equity, by providing insights into how women navigate a patriarchal and at times paternalistic work terrain, but also that the recommendations at the end of the monograph will be useful for global readers too (both policy makers and scholars).

To sum up, in the context of an ever-expanding industry that is seeing tectonic shifts, it is anticipated that this monograph will provide a deeper understanding for the reader of the existing scenario by penetrating the surface of everyday practices and discourses, to reveal deeply embedded practices, viewpoints and biases.

Payal Kumar

Author of the following related titles:

- *Gender Equity in the Boardroom: The Case of India.* Emerald Group Publishing, 2020 (Co-author Dr Ganesh Singh)
- *Mentorship-driven Talent Management: The Asian Experience.* Emerald Group Publishing, 2020 (Co-author Prof. Pawan Budhwar)
- *Exploring Dynamic Mentoring Models in India.* Springer International Publishing, 2018.
- *Indian Women as Entrepreneurs: An Exploration of Self-identity.* Springer International Publishing, 2016.
- *Unveiling Women's Leadership: Identity and Meaning of Leadership in India.* Springer International Publishing, 2015.

Acknowledgements

I must acknowledge the leadership of the Indian School of Hospitality (ISH), Gurugram, India, represented by Mr Dilip Puri, Founder and CEO, and also Mr Kunal Vasudeva, Co-founder and COO. Had they not brought me into the lap of the ISH family and introduced me to the world of hospitality, this book would never have materialized. Further wings were provided by those at the helm of the Women's Indian Chamber of Commerce and Industry, who encouraged me to write the white paper that preceded this book.

Chapter 1

Tourism and Hospitality: Pre- and Post-COVID-19 Pandemic

The tourism and hospitality industry – one of the major contributors to the world economy – is exceptionally people-centric. In the editorial of *The State of Hospitality – Insight Report* published by Sommet Education, March 2022, the CEO of Sommet Education Benoît-Etienne Domenget writes,

> Hospitality is more than a business. It's a community of contemporary nomads sharing the same curiosity for travel, an openness to different cultures, the attention to detail, the willingness to welcome and please others.[1]

This industry is quite vast, broadly comprising the following sub-categories: lodging, including a range of properties from luxury hotels, to bed and breakfasts, to camping grounds; food and beverage, which includes establishments that sell food and drinks for consumption on or off premises; recreation, which includes venues for entertainment and relaxation, such as theme parks, theatres, etc.; and travel and tourism, including airlines and cruises.

Before the pandemic, at a global level, the travel and tourism sector alone accounted for 10.4% of the global gross domestic product (GDP; USD 9.2 trillion), 6.8% of the total exports, or 27.4% of the global services exports in the form of international visitor spending. This sector created one out of every four new jobs, accounting for 10.6% of all jobs. This sector took a big hit due to the COVID-19 pandemic, suffering a loss of approximately USD 4.5 trillion in 2020, with its contribution to the global GDP declining by a massive 49.1%, with job losses amounting to 62 million worldwide.[2]

---

[1]*The State of Hospitality 2022 – Insight Report* published by Sommet Education – March 2022. file:///C:/Users/ish080/Downloads/The%20State%20of%20Hospitality%202022%20-%20LD%20(3).pdf, accessed on 6 January 2023.
[2]https://wttc.org/Research/Economic-Impact, accessed on 21 December 2022.

Gender Equity in Hospitality: The Case of India, 1–11
Copyright © 2023 by Payal Kumar
Published under exclusive licence by Emerald Publishing Limited
doi:10.1108/978-1-80382-665-320231001

Today the room for growth is tremendous.[3] The United Nations (UN) World Tourism Organization forecasts 1.8 billion international tourists by 2030. One area that is growing rapidly is sustainable tourism, or the adoption of responsible practices by the tourism industry by acknowledging both its negative and positive impacts, eventually maximizing the positives and minimizing the negatives. The notable positive aspects of sustainable tourism include employment generation, preservation of natural and cultural heritage, and monumental restoration. Some potential negatives are climate change, overcrowding at popular destinations, damage to environment and heritage properties, excessive energy consumption, and economic leakage. So important is sustainable tourism that in the UN's Sustainable Development goals target 8.9, the aim is to devise and implement policies by 2030 to promote sustainable tourism that creates jobs and also promotes local culture.

In the financial year 2019–2020, the Indian travel and tourism industry was ranked 10th in the world, among 185 countries with respect to contribution to the GDP. It contributed 6.8% of the country's total GDP and accounted for 8% of the total employment, which is around 39 million jobs. According to estimates, this number will rise up to 53 million jobs by 2029.[4]

Even in pre-pandemic times, the industry faced a unique set of challenges that impacted the number of foreign tourist arrivals (FTAs) in India. In 2019, India attracted 17.91 million FTAs, compared to even smaller countries that were far ahead, for example, Italy (64.5 million), Turkey (51.2 million), Mexico (45 million), and Thailand (39.8 million).[5] The lack of infrastructure, connectivity, cleanliness, pollution, health, and safety are stated to be the primary reasons for the low FTAs in India. Furthermore, India is perceived as an expensive country in comparison to others such as Thailand, Cambodia, and Sri Lanka.

Another possible reason is that campaigns such as 'Incredible India' may have led to a stereotypical image of the country as a spiritual destination to find one's true self and attain Nirvana, which could be underplaying India as a destination for scenic landscapes and wildlife, eco-tourism, and rural tourism. There is a huge untapped potential for India to also go to the sustainable tourism way, defined as 'tourism that takes full account of its current and future economic, social and environmental impacts, addressing the needs of visitors, the industry, the environment and host communities' (UNEP & WTO, 2005, p. 12).

India withstood two debilitating waves of COVID-19, but these and the subsequent lock-downs had a disastrous impact both economically and in terms of huge job losses in tourism and hospitality. There were estimated job losses of 14.5 million in 2020's first quarter alone. The industry was caught completely unaware,

---

[3]See Fig. 1.
[4]https://www.ibef.org/industry/tourism-hospitality-india, accessed on 17 January 2023.
[5]https://www.statista.com/statistics/305501/number-of-international-tourist-arrivals-in-india/, accessed on 20 December 2022.

and managers were perplexed as to what to do in the face of such a calamity (Ghosh & Bhattacharya, 2022; Kaushal & Srivastava, 2020).

Due to financial distress, some travel agencies were delisted and there was also a mass firing of employees in many hotels. However, this knee-jerk reaction backfired to some extent once the lockdown was over, as many of the ex-employees opted to join other industries rather than return to the hospitality sector, leading to a severe talent crunch. Said Gautam Srivastava, Vice President HR, The Leela Palaces, Hotels and Resorts,

> Attracting talent was always a problem, but this has been aggravated post-pandemic. In the pandemic many hotels let go of up to 30% of their employees. Many now don't want to return because of other opportunities.

He was speaking at the 2022 Hotel Operations Summit – India, at a panel discussion on 'In Search of Talent' moderated by Prahlad Puri, Co-Founder & Executive Director, Indian School of Hospitality (ISH).[6] Other panellists included Ashutosh Khanna, industry HR Expert; Nikhil Sharma, Regional Director, Eurasia at Wyndham Hotels & Resorts; Shiv Agrawal, MD, ABC consultants; and Yogendra Agnihotri, Senior Director Human Resources South Asia at Radisson Hotel Group. The discussion centred around several key points, as follows:

- Today's generation seeks empowerment and freedom in their work as they have multiple opportunities to choose from. It is time to accept that this is a problem that needs more than lip service from the industry.
- Compensation has to be brought to an acceptable level that compares with other industries. Even some start-ups are paying better.
- Work–life balance needs to be looked at, as shift work at hotels is still very regimented.
- It's the first time in the industry that all three generations are working together: Gen Y, X, and Z. It is essential to invest in people managers so they can manage the expectations of all the generations.
- Many fresh hospitality graduates are more attracted to other sectors such as retail, healthcare, and e-commerce such as Amazon.

Dilip Puri, founder and CEO of the ISH, Gurgaon, reiterates these sentiments by saying that leaders are realizing that the industry needs to change the way that human capital is treated in order to stem talent drain, for example, by rationalizing work hours and hiking pay.

> I think COVID has been a big teacher for our industry. The industry recognizes that it needs to pay more. I'm already beginning to

---

[6]https://www.youtube.com/watch?v=m20F_6bhG_U&t=2641s, accessed on 20 December 2022.

see in a lot of companies a very major effort being made towards pay parity with other competing industries.[7]

In a recent survey conducted on a sample of 170 students of a leading hospitality school regarding their internship experience across leading hotels of international and domestic brands operating in India, only 35% of students expressed a continued willingness to join the industry (see Appendix Table A1). The desire to join other sectors was linked to reputation, payment, and faster growth opportunities. It is increasingly evident that Gen Z, who are on the brink of entering the workforce, have a lot more choices available to them, and that they are willing to weigh these choices before making a final career decision.

Here are what some students said about aspiring to join other industries:

• 'My career aspirations are still not on a single decision. I would like to experience more in the industry and aligned industries to find out where my interests are.'
• 'Long working hours and working conditions put me off a career in hospitality.'
• 'I would like to step into the corporate world and might join a marketing firm.'
• 'My long-term goal is an entrepreneurial journey, but I would like to start in the marketing domain, across industries.'
• 'My career aspiration now is to work in a corporate bank.'

To sum up, in the post-pandemic era, while there is definitely a boom in the tourism and hospitality industry in India, especially with the expansion of the e-visa scheme to 171 countries, there are still several workforce issues that need to be ironed out such as employee attrition, long working hours, fair compensation, gender equity issues, and talent drain due to the opening up of diverse alternative opportunities for the workforce. In-depth research on these topics is critical, both to build on existing scholarship and also because these challenges have a strong bearing on the growth of the industry as a continued economic driver for the nation.

The Global Gender Gap

While the global gender gap and also leadership challenges for women to reach the top may seem to be high in South Asian countries like India, a systematic literature review of papers between 1990 and 2021 suggests that barriers faced by women in both developing and developed countries are quite similar (Kulkarni & Mishra, 2022). Furthermore, even in developed countries such as the United States, it's not necessarily a rosy picture. In fact, here there are other challenges such as an increasing trend for woman leaders to change jobs at the highest rate

[7]https://hospitality.economictimes.indiatimes.com/news/hotels/hotels-will-start-paying-better-and-rationalising-working-hours-soon-dilip-puri/94931596

ever, as per a recent McKinsey report on 'Women at the workplace, 2022'.[8] The reasons range from microaggressions, to seeking a work culture which allows for more flexibility and/or remote work.

Gender parity is a global concern, and it is women who bear the brunt of inequities. In fact, there is a gap of 31.9% at the global level that needs to be addressed in order to achieve gender parity globally, but it will take 132 years to do so (World Economic Forum (WEF), 2022). Women are politically disadvantaged because of lack of representation in parliaments, where women occupy only 25% of seats and governments, and account for 21% of ministerships. Moreover, 85 countries of the 153 countries studied in this report have not elected female heads of state in the last 50 years. At the same time, while there has been an increase in the number of women in senior roles, women's participation in the labour market is low (55%) in comparison with men (78%).

A wage gap of 40% and an income gap of more than 50% also need to be addressed. In some countries, women find it difficult to begin entrepreneurial ventures because of a lack of access to resources such as finance, land, and credit. All these factors lead to widening financial disparities between men and women.

The report estimates that South Asia, having closed only 35.7% of the gender gap, will take 197 years to achieve gender parity. The subindices economic participation and opportunity (35.7%) and political empowerment (26.3%) contribute to the gender disparities in this region (WEF, 2022). India, the largest country in this region, geographically and economically, is ranked at 135 out of 146 countries with only 62.9% of the gender gap closed. In comparison, Bangladesh is ranked 71 with 71.4% of the gap addressed. The least performing country in the region is Afghanistan, which is ranked 146, with 43.5% parity achieved.

The subindices in India are similar to other countries in South Asia as a whole, including low participation of women in the labour force, leading to a lack of economic and financial independence, and also political disempowerment leading to a lack of proper representation in the corridors of power. Of particular concern is the fact that women's participation in the labour force has been on the decline over the past few decades. According to data from the World Bank, the female labour force participation rate (FLFPR) in India has seen a decline from 30.27% in 1990 to 20.8% in 2019.

Another important finding from the report is that globally the jobs performed by men and women have become gendered. For instance, domains such as cloud computing, engineering, and data and artificial intelligence are mostly for male, while domains that involve people and culture such as teaching are more for female. Furthermore, an extremely significant aspect of women's economic participation is that they are often engaged in work that is undervalued and largely invisible, while overall putting in more hours than that of men at the workplace.

Furthermore, women in leadership positions are few and far between. India is ranked *135 out* of a total 146 countries on the index of the WEF Global Gender

---

[8]https://www.mckinsey.com/featured-insights/diversity-and-inclusion/women-in-the-workplace

Gap,[9] which is hardly becoming of a nation which has risen to the ranks of the fifth largest economy in the world, having overtaken the United Kingdom. In my Emerald Publishers book that preceded this one, namely *Gender Equity in the Boardroom: The Case of India* (2020), co-authored with Dr Ganesh Singh, we examined female boardroom representation to try and understand why the number of women in the corporate boardroom was still less than international numbers, in spite of affirmative action in which the Companies Act (2013) prescribes that at least one female director needs to be appointed to company boards in India for every listed company and also for every public company with a turnover of 3 billion INR or more. In our study, we found that even if women were represented as board members, they were often a family member of the founder of the company instead of independent director candidates.

We found barriers to growth at three levels of analysis. For example, at the individual level, some women felt there was an uneven playing field when it came to biology, with women having to take time out for childbirth and childcare. At the group level, there appears to be more networking exposure for men, which is very important for selection on corporate boards. Finally, at the firm level of analysis, it was found that some leaders were paternalistic which hindered career growth (e.g. not sending women to remote locations in an effort to protect their safety), and that there were also less mentorship opportunities.

Women were disproportionately affected by the pandemic as per the Global Gender Gap Report (WEF, 2022). For example, in India, women lost jobs at a higher rate, while domestic violence soared to unprecedented levels. The then President of India, Ram Nath Kovind, openly acknowledged in a letter to young Indians how women in India were put under a triple burden due to the pandemic. They did paid work, unpaid work, and also had to tutor their children who were now doing online classes from the confines of their homes. He wrote, ' … as children attend school from home, their learning has to be supplemented by the parents, and that task usually falls on the mother'.[10]

Women in the Tourism and Hospitality Industry

According to the Global Report on Women in Tourism (UNWTO, 2019), 54% of the workforce employed in the tourism industry are women, with a pay gap of 14.7% between men and women. In the Asia-Pacific too, women account for 53% of the tourism workforce. However, most women are employed in this industry perform jobs with poor working conditions and pay. Also, women are more constrained by traditional gender norms and roles, in comparison with men, which dictate what women can or cannot do, whether they can or cannot work.

---

[9]https://www.weforum.org/reports/global-gender-gap-report-2022/, accessed on 21 December 2022.
[10]https://indiaeducationdiary.in/kfc-india-extends-growth-opportunities-for-women-leaders-with-their-first-area-coaches-programme-for-women/, accessed on 8 November 2022.

Cultural traditions, which prescribe traditional gender roles in the home and workplace, combine with workplace cultures and expectations in tourism that disadvantage women who aspire to a reasonable balance between work and family (child and elder) care responsibilities. (UNWTO, 2019, p. 96)

In Asia, in general, gender parity has never been a key discussion point in tourism policies and industry events, whereas technology and economy always are. In addition, data are also not available for all sectors of the tourism and hospitality industry, and whatever is available cannot be generalized for the whole of the continent, because of the diversity between the various regions and sub-regions. Yet, tourism can play a critical role in achieving the commitments at the core of the 2030 Agenda for Sustainable Development – gender equality, women's empowerment, and inclusive development (UNWTO, 2019).

Women do, however, have the option of pursuing entrepreneurial ventures in the tourism sector, even in rural areas, and they can do so with moderate start-up financing (International Finance Corporation (IFC), 2017). The road to entrepreneurship, however, brings forth its own challenges. There are several constraints, namely inadequate access to collateral, financing, markets, technology, information, business skills, and education and training (IFC, 2017). In spite of women preferring to hire other women in management roles in their businesses, the 'ideal worker' stereotype in the tourism and hospitality industry is still considered as male, which hampers women's career progression (Costa, Bakas, Breda, Durão, Carvalho, et al., 2017).

The Castell Project has been tracking corporate performance in terms of gender diversity, mostly in the US and Canadian hospitality management, by means of its annual report among other initiatives. According to The Castell Project (2020) report, overall women held 12% of the leadership roles in the hospitality industry, such as 'chief, managing director, president, partner, principal, and CEO' (p. 3). Women perform leadership roles mostly in areas such as accounting, human resources, legal, marketing, and revenue management departments. What is of particular concern, however, is the fact that while at the manager, director, and vice president level, men and women are fairly evenly poised, it becomes tougher for women to break the glass ceiling to attain roles as partner/principal, C-suite leader, managing director, or president. In fact, the odds of women achieving CEO roles are one woman to 20.4 men. There were no comparable reports found for South Asia.

It is evident from all the aforementioned reports that women across the world face systemic, deeply entrenched problems. In the tourism and hospitality industry in particular, these disadvantages are reflected in the status of women – low pay, low status jobs at the entry level, stagnation in the middle management levels, and barriers on the way to boardrooms and senior executive roles to name a few. There is, therefore, a lot of ground to cover in order to achieve gender parity at multiple levels.

One noticeable trend in the hospitality industry in India which deserves further study is gender equity – or the lack of it – given the apparent preference for men in senior positions and younger women at lower levels (Chaudhary & Gupta, 2010) in a country that is high in patriarchy and masculinity. As per Hofstede's (2001) dimensions,

> Masculinity stands for a society in which social gender roles are clearly distinct: Men are supposed to be assertive, tough, and focused on material success; women are supposed to be more modest, tender, and concerned with the quality of life. (p. 297)

Said Meena Bhatia, Vice President and General Manager of Le Meridien New Delhi,

> Coming from the baby boomer generation, we were faced with not only lack of opportunities, but lack of social acceptance for careers in hospitality. The role of women in hospitality was often misconstrued; the space was male dominated with the exception of a few trivial positions that could be occupied by men.[11]

Common prejudices in the industry include the perception that women are not to cope with the pressure of long office hours, night shifts, nor are able to maintain a healthy work–life interface (Sharma & Kaur, 2019). To compound these prejudices, there are other obstacles to woman's leadership advancement such as less developmental training compared to male counterparts, and also cultural discouragement (Patwardhan, Mayya, & Joshi, 2016). Conscious and unconscious biases that are associated with gendered culture and discriminatory practices seem to be prevalent in most industries (Maheshwari & Lenka, 2022). No recent research has been conducted on why less female representation in leadership roles still exists for women in the hospitality sector in India, hence this study.

Objectives of the Study

Research on gender issues within the tourism and hospitality industry has not been as substantial as in other areas such as history, sociology, or management studies. And yet, the need for understanding gender challenges and opportunities in hospitality research and education is substantial (Morgan & Pritchard, 2019). In the past, questions about gender have been dismissed as a minority concern (Oakley, 2006) or as disruptive (Tribe, 2010).

Moreover, the myth of gender neutrality is perpetuated by making gender invisible.

> Gender neutrality is such a widely accepted practice in business that women, and anyone else who feels they do not really fit into the

---

[11]https://hospitality.economictimes.indiatimes.com/news/speaking-heads/let-us-think-and-act-differently/81391004, accessed on 21 December 2022.

dominant practices and preferred behaviours, blames this on themselves and not on the exclusionary consequences of the masculine
norm of the ideal worker and organization. (Dashper, 2019, p. 4)

This study delves into gender equity concerns pertaining to hospitality industry of India. There have been only a few academic studies focussing on this topic,
therefore the literature surveyed in this study pertains mostly to countries in
Europe, the United States, and South-east Asia. In fact, research on gender and
leadership has been dominated by the west, where there are more women leaders than in developing countries (Kulkarni & Mishra, 2022). However, scholars
are increasingly questioning whether or not this presents us with the full picture
on gendered leadership. Furthermore, scholars are increasingly questioning the
positivist trend of decontextualizing leadership studies from the socio-cultural
context of the workplace.

This study adds to the literature of the Global South by highlighting the
contextual differences of barriers to woman leadership in the Indian hospitality
sector – a country known to be a patriarchal and a high-power distance society
country. An example of a gendered role is that in India, and in fact in most South
Asian countries, women are expected to take a break in their careers after childbirth (Bhattacharya, Mohapatra, & Bhattacharya, 2018). It is envisaged that policy recommendations would differ in the cultural context of different countries,

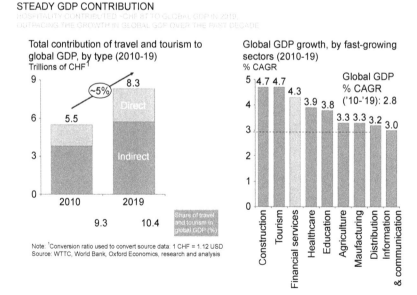

Fig. 1.   Steady Growth and Global GDP Contribution of Travel and Tourism.
Source: The State of Hospitality 2022 – Insight Report published by Sommet
Education – March 2022. file:///C:/Users/ish080/Downloads/The%20State%20
of%20Hospitality%202022%20-%20LD%20(3).pdf, accessed on 6 January 2023.

given that gender is a social structure, which is constructed at the 'level of individual identities, cultural expectations embedded into interaction, and institutional opportunities and constraints' (Risman, 2004, p. 444).

Prior to this monograph, an approach study was written by this author, sponsored by Women's Indian Chamber of Commerce & Industry *(WICCI)* in collaboration with the Indian ISH, India. This was launched by the Additional Director General of the Ministry of Tourism, Government of India, Ms Rupinder Brar, on 10 March 2022 at Le Meridian Hotel, New Delhi.

Kanika Hasrat, National President of WICCI Tourism and Hospitality and Area Director UP, MP, and Uttarakhand and General Manager at Taj Lakefront Bhopal at The Indian Hotel Company Limited, said

> I would encourage the industry to review this study on 'Evaluation of the state of Gender Equity in India's Hospitality Industry' with a keen eye. It will help us work together to recalibrate our businesses and make them truly inclusive. The women at WICCI Tourism and hospitality are aligned to work with industry partners to build focused conversations, provide mentoring opportunities, offer a level playing field for women and instill a culture of diversity in leadership. It is with this clear and ultimate goal of more women in leadership that we will all thrive.[12]

(Left to Right), Kanika Hasrat, Rupinder Brar, Payal Kumar, and Dilip Puri. At the Launch of the Approach Study, March 2022, New Delhi, India.

---

[12]https://www.hotelierindia.com/events/wicci-hospitality-tourism-and-indian-school-of-hospitality-launch-a-whitepaper

It is hoped that this monograph will be useful for various types of readership:

- For diversity and inclusion scholar and also critical management scholars and educators around the world, this book will be an ideal case study for understanding contextual differences of barriers to woman leadership in a patriarchal and high-power distance society. How can women achieve gender equity or 'fairness of treatment' in terms of rights, benefits, and opportunities, in a society that expects the woman to be the primary care-giver at home too? How can women overcome gender stereotypes of not being suitable for leadership roles in the hospitality industry?
- This study will also provide important insights for leaders in the hospitality industry by showcasing barriers to gender equity, both systemic and individual. There are also details of enablers and success stories of good HR policies for women, including flexi-timing, that could be emulated by these leaders.
- The study findings are likely to be useful as a stepping-stone for policy makers, and industry leaders to rebound from the pandemic to transform India into one of the top 20 tourist destinations in the world.
- It is hoped that the policy recommendations at the end of the study will lead to positive action by the Indian Government, which could possibly enable India to rise a few notches in the global gender gap index.

Chapter 2

Literature Review

There is evidence to show that there are positive financial outcomes of a diverse leadership. For example, studies suggest that greater female board representation has a positive impact on the firm's market performance in those countries with greater gender parity (Post & Byron, 2015). Furthermore, McKinsey & Company (2020) reported a differential of 48% in performance between the most and the least gender-diverse companies. Another report, the result of a longitudinal study on Russell 3000 index companies carried out over 17 years, found that companies with female chief executive officers (CEOs) and chief financial officers (CFOs) performed better on stock prices in comparison with the market average. This report too broadly states that companies with highly gender-diverse boards of directors are larger and more profitable than firms with low gender diversity (S&P Global, 2019).

There are also positive non-financial outcomes of gender-diverse leadership. Diverse teams are more likely to pursue extensive innovation, foresee changes in consumer needs and trends, and aid companies in gaining a competitive edge (LeanIn.org & McKinsey, 2019). Woman leaders tend to be transformational in nature, so they are 'thus more focused on those aspects of leadership that predict effectiveness' (Eagly, Johannesen-Schmidt, & van Engen, 2003, p. 586). Female leaders tend to value others' contributions, and reward subordinates for performance, which are great performance motivators (Korn Ferry Institute, 2017).

In spite of these significant positive outcomes of gender diversity, women continue to remain underrepresented in the upper echelons of management. Scholars have described this phenomenon using several metaphors, the most common of which is 'glass ceiling'. The term is used to describe the invisible barriers that women encounter on the way to the executive suite. Carvalho, Costa, Lykke, Torres, and Wahl (2018) find that the 'glass ceiling' effects persist even at the top. Participants in their study have talked of how they have had their authority defied and have also struggled to be heard.

The 'glass elevator' is the term used to describe the subtle, invisible advantages that men working in occupations typically considered 'female', like nursing and teaching, apparently benefit from including faster promotion (Williams, 1992). And 'glass cliff' is the phenomenon used to describe a scenario where women are placed in leadership roles during negative financial situations, thus endangering their positions (Ryan & Haslam, 2005).

Gender Equity in Hospitality: The Case of India, 13–23
Copyright © 2023 by Payal Kumar
Published under exclusive licence by Emerald Publishing Limited
doi:10.1108/978-1-80382-665-320231002

LeanIn.org and McKinsey' (2019) report the use of the term 'broken rung' to describe the problem of the lack of qualified women ready or available to take on leadership roles (also known as the leaky pipeline problem). According to the report, the root cause of the problem lies in the fact that for 'every 100 men promoted and hired to manager, only 72 women are hired and promoted' (p. 11). This inequality results in women being stuck at the entry/junior level, leading to a lesser number of women managers. As the number of women at every successive level decreases further, men continue to outnumber women. Thus, women do not get the opportunity to catch up at all.

Gender and the various aspects of its representation have been extensively researched in management domains, with considerable focus on discrimination on the basis of gender (Cleveland, Vescio, & Barnes-Farnell, 2005). Based on the findings from the broader management research and the specific research on the tourism and hospitality industry, several themes and subthemes can be discerned, as represented in Table 1.

Gender Stereotypes and Prejudices

Gender stereotypes are generalizations derived from the attributed qualities of men and women. They may be classified as descriptive – what men or women are like; or prescriptive – how men and women ought to be (Heilman, 2012). Eagly and Karau (2002) describe two types of attributes: 'agentic' which signifies a tendency for assertiveness, control, and confidence, and 'communal' which imply concern with the welfare of other people, like kindness, gentleness, sympathy, and nurturing. Men are perceived to possess agentic attributes, and women communal. A leader is said to exhibit 'agentic' attributes, which means that men, more than women, fit the cultural constructs of leadership. The result of gender stereotyping can be twofold: (a) in comparison with men, women are deemed to be less effective as potential leaders, and (b) the behaviour expected from a leader is unfavourably judged when performed by a woman (Eagly & Karau, 2002).

In other words, women face a competency 'double bind' with reference to leadership roles. If women leaders exhibit behaviour consistent with female stereotypes, then they are considered to be 'too soft' or less competent leaders, but they can get labelled as 'too tough' if they exhibit behaviour inconsistent with gender stereotypes. Women are required to prove their leadership abilities and manage expectations constantly, but are judged according to much higher standards as compared with men (Catalyst, 2007).

The 'maternal wall' denotes a specific form of stereotyping that adversely affects successful women if they are pregnant, or draw on maternal leave or other flexible working solutions. Potential consequences may include negative performance evaluation and lack of support.

> Managers and coworkers may mentally cloak pregnant women and new mothers in a haze of femininity, assuming they will be empathetic, emotional, gentle, non-aggressive – that is, not very good at business. (Williams, 2004, p. 3)

Table 1.   Themes and Subthemes on Gender Equity from the Literature.

Theme	Subtheme	Selected Publications
Gender stereotypes and prejudices	Qualities attributed to men and women; challenges faced by woman leaders	Eagly and Karau (2002), Catalyst (2007), Koenig, Eagly, Mitchell, and Ristikari (2011); Heilman (2012), and Eagly, Nater, Miller, Kaufmann, and Sczesny (2020)
	Maternal wall	Williams (2004), Cuddy, Fiske, and Glick (2004), McIntosh McQuaid, Munro, and Dabir-Alai (2012), Costa, Bakas, Breda, Durão, Carvalho, et al. (2017), and Dashper (2019)
	Pitfalls in workplace negotiation	Lauterbach and Weiner (1996), Babcock and Laschever (2003, 2008), Bowles, Babcock, and McGinn (2005), Bowles, Babcock, and Lai (2007), LeanIn.org and McKinsey (2016), and Bligh and Ito (2017)
Tourism and hospitality industry	Working conditions	Guerrier and Adib (2000), Hoel and Einarsen (2003), Baum (2007), Mooney and Ryan (2009), Morgan and Pritchard (2018), and Ranjith Kumara (2018)
	Stereotypes in the tourism and hospitality industry	Hicks (1990), Purcell (1996), Dashper (2019), Mooney, Ryan, and Harris (2017), Costa, Bakas, Breda, Durão, Carvalho, et al. (2017), Costa, Bakas, Breda, and Durão (2017)
	Gender-based segregation	Ng and Pine (2003), Kattara (2005), Santos and Varejão (2007), Chaudhary and Gupta (2010), Campos-Soria, García-Pozo, and Sánchez-Ollero (2011, 2015), Carvalho, Costa, Lykke, and Torres (2019)

(Continued)

Table 1. (*Continued*)

Theme	Subtheme	Selected Publications
	Gender pay gap	Bertrand and Hallock (2001); Crosby, Williams, and Biernat (2004), Skalpe (2007), Thrane (2008), Muñoz-Bullón (2009), Campos-Soria, Ortega-Aguaza, and Ropero-García (2009), England (2010), Fleming (2015), England Bearak, Budig, and Hodges (2016), Ferreira Freire Guimarães and Silva (2016), and Marfil Cotilla and Campos-Soria (2021)
	Other organizational barriers	Brownell (1994), Lyness and Thompson (2000), Li and Wang-Leung (2001), Lyness and Schrader (2006), Huffman, Cohen, and Pearlman (2010), King et al. (2012), Boone et al. (2013), and Karunarathna (2015)
Work–life interface	Stereotypes of and expectations from the 'ideal worker'	Hochschild (1997), Williams (2000), Galinsky and Matos (2011), Davies and Frink (2014), Reid and Ramarajan (2016), Kumar and Singh (2020), and Kumar, Chakraborty, and Kumar (2020)
	Social reproductive economy: childcare and eldercare	Bakker (2007), Blair-Loy (2003), Leslie Manchester, Park, and Mehng (2012), and Morgan and Pritchard (2018)
	Tourism and hospitality industry attributes of 'flexibility' and availability for work	McIntosh et al. (2012) and Segovia-Pérez, Figueroa-Domecq, Fuentes-Moraleda, and Muñoz-Mazón (2019)

Source: Author's own.

Mothers of young children are often unable to embody the masculine norm of the ideal worker in hospitality, who is able to commit to work above all else and be constantly available to respond to the organization's needs 24×7 (Costa, Bakas, Breda, Durão, Carvalho, et al., 2017).

Women resuming work after maternity may feel the need to take back their previously held positions because of feelings of displacement since 'the organization may have moved on and developed without them' (Costa, Bakas, Breda, Durão, Carvalho, et al., 2017, p. 5). The most affected are usually part-time employees, since utilizing flexible work times is perceived to be a lack of commitment and hence such workers are not seen as suitable for senior management roles (Dashper, 2019). Motherhood remains a barrier to career progression even in professions like nursing, which is gendered female and is female-dominated (McIntosh et al., 2012). In another study, Cuddy et al. (2004) suggest that mothers were deemed to be less competent than fathers and/or employees without children.

When gender stereotypes and roles are internalized through repeated conditioning and reinforcement, women at times impose certain restrictions on themselves. The report *Women in the Workplace* states that when women ask for better opportunities, they often face social backlash – and are considered 'bossy' or 'aggressive', and so they often don't ask but prefer to remain silent (LeanIn.org & McKinsey, 2016). Research also suggests that there is less likelihood of women negotiating an equitable salary and perks, more challenging work assignments, and even promotions (Babcock, Gelfand, Small, & Stayn, 2006). Results from a study conducted by Exley, Niederle, and Vesterlund (2016) show that when there is a higher probability of negative consequences, women may refrain from negotiating altogether, especially as male evaluators may punish women who ask for higher salaries in comparison with their male colleagues. Organizations prefer leaders who negotiate for better opportunities, promotions, assignments, etc., but they do not particularly encourage negotiation from women. Thus, women stand to lose out on better opportunities, and the gaps between men and women increase, leading to an underrepresentation of women in leadership roles.

The most sought-after attributes of leaders in the hospitality industry are willingness to work long hours, be mobile, self-promote, and network (Dashper, 2019). These attributes are considered to be gender neutral. However, these norms are so deeply gendered as masculine that managers 'may be embedded within the masculine norm of managerial discourse to such an extent that they do not realize it' (Costa et al., 2017, p. 152).

This is echoed in an earlier study conducted on hospitality managers based in the United Kingdom (Hicks, 1990). The findings from the study indicate deeply entrenched beliefs about the attributes of a successful operations manager in the industry, which were invariably 'male' along with stereotypical views about the supposed shortcomings of women's traits and attitudes towards work. Such stereotypical beliefs can have wide-ranging effects on the career aspirations of women, from influencing recruitment decisions to excluding women from opportunities based on the flawed rationale of inappropriateness of women in management roles.

Variables in the Hospitality Industry

Working conditions: The hospitality industry is primarily a service industry. Some employees like housekeeping require direct interaction with clients, whereas others like kitchen and maintenance staff do not. A successful hotel needs to ensure that frontline employees do everything possible to satisfy clients, which often means long, irregular working hours, including working in the evenings and nights, and even on Sundays and during festivals (Hoel & Einarsen, 2003). Part-time or temporary contracts are a common practice in the hospitality industry, more so for unskilled women (Campos-Soria et al., 2015).

Frontline hotel staff are susceptible to violence and sexual harassment, which could be verbal – in the form of obscene language and jokes, and suggestive jokes, to the more physical – like groping, touching, slapping, and kissing (Morgan & Pritchard, 2018). The problem is exacerbated in restaurants, bars, casinos, and nightclubs in hospitality and in the airline sector too, because of the sexualization of women who are employed in these establishments in the form of uniforms that emphasize their attractiveness, and in the way they are 'encouraged to flirt and "sell" their sexuality in service encounters' (Morgan & Pritchard, 2018, p. 4).

Work mobility: Career progression in the hotel industry is dependent on continuous employment and a certain degree of mobility, both between departments and between geographical locations. The ideal hotel manager acquires competencies pertaining to several departments. This internal mobility is considered to be a positive feature in the hospitality industry, leading to better opportunities and salary rewards (Ranjith Kumara, 2018). There is a difference between how men and women deal with the issue of mobility. Men change jobs often and assume more management roles before reaching the level of general manager (Blayney & Blotnicky, 2010), whereas women tend to remain with the same company in order to keep their social capital intact (Mooney & Ryan, 2009). This means that they make fewer career moves and may find it difficult to achieve senior management roles.

Gender-based segregation: The hospitality industry, like other industries, too exhibits gender stereotyping. Much of hospitality work is considered to be 'women's work' since it consists of activities which are traditionally performed by women in homes (Morgan & Pritchard, 2018). Horizontal and vertical segregation is still prevalent in the industry with evidence from several countries, for example, the United Kingdom, Egypt and the Middle East, Hong Kong, Spain and India, among others. Vertical segregation means that the majority of the general managers are men, whereas women form the majority of low- to mid-level management. As for horizontal segregation, even when women are promoted to departmental head levels, the departments they handle are mostly housekeeping, personnel, and training, whereas their male counterparts handle departments such as food and beverage and finance (Ng & Pine, 2003).

There are other patterns of gender segregation, for instance: (a) gender segregation increases with workers' age and the size of the establishment. But decreases with education levels of the workers, (b) this seems to be more common with part-time and seasonal workers, (c) in the hotel industry, horizontal segregation is more prevalent than vertical segregation, whereas both horizontal and vertical segregation are prevalent in restaurants, and (d) horizontal segregation increases and vertical segregation decreases with increase in the size of the establishment. In a study by Ng and Pine (2003), the findings indicate that while men were comfortable with female subordinates, they were not comfortable working with female supervisors.

Huffman et al. (2010) found that gender segregation may be less if women have influence over the hiring process. Dezsö, Ross, and Uribe (2016) found that while women may help other women, it may not be sufficient to counteract the resistance from male managers.

Pay gap: Countries around the world have enacted legislation that guarantees 'equal pay for equal work' for individuals and prohibits discrimination on any grounds, for example, Equal Remuneration Act, 1976 (2021) in India, and the Equality Act, 2010 (2021) in the United Kingdom. In spite of such affirmative action, the pay gap between men and women persists. Research conducted across the United States and Europe attempts to explain the gender pay gap in general, and in hospitality management in particular. Theoretical explanations of the gender pay gap generally fall into two categories, those offering 'legitimate' reasons for the disparity (i.e. justified by economic or other non-discriminatory factors) and those identifying discrimination as the explanation (Fleming, 2015, p. 181). The first category consists of the human capital theory, which posits that individuals at different levels of education, training, or experience, will have different levels of productivity and therefore, different pay levels; and the new home economics theory which states that people devote different amounts of time to paid work will have different levels of productivity, and therefore, different pay levels. Fleming (2015) states that according to these two theories, if men and women work different numbers of hours and possess different levels of education, training, and experience, then the observable gaps in pay levels between genders make economic sense.

The second category consists of the theories of occupational overcrowding, evaluation of female work, and social closure. The occupation overcrowding theory (Bergmann, 1974) posits that men and women are segregated into gendered jobs, reducing the number of jobs available to women. Therefore, when the supply of labour exceeds demand, the wage rate shows a corresponding decrease. In the context of evaluation of female work, England (2010) states that when employees devalue women's work on the basis of gender stereotypes, they often set lower wage levels for both men and women occupied in 'female' occupations.

Fleming's (2015) study, based on data collected from the hospitality industry in the United States, shows a significant difference between the compensation of men and women, in spite of the increasing number of women in professional and executive positions in general and in the hospitality industry in particular. Variables for human capital, new home economics, and overcrowding were only able to partially explain the gender pay gap. The highest levels of unexplained gender pay gap were reported at the managerial level.

Ferreira Freire Guimarães and Silva (2016) find that entrenched gender discrimination exists in the Brazilian tourism industry, with women receiving lesser compensation than men, even when they possess similar characteristics and work similar jobs. They noticed both vertical and horizontal job segregation, with women concentrated in low-paying jobs that are perceived to be 'feminine'. Santos and Varejao (2007) found that the gender pay gap in the tourism and hospitality industry in Portugal was caused by occupational segregation (45%) and discrimination (55%). There is more vertical segregation in Portugal rather than horizontal, considering the fact women comprised only 29.9% of senior management. About 45% of the gender pay gap in the hospitality industry in Portugal could be explained by the differences in the characteristics of male and female employees. The unexplained gap of 55% was attributed to discrimination. Further analysis reveals that the pay gap was caused because of the fact that men were 'paid above the non-discriminating wage structure' (p. 237), thus, benefitting the male employees more than the female employees.

Muñoz-Bullón (2009) found a pay gap of 6.7% in the Spanish tourism industry. The primary cause of this gap, according to this study, is the type of contracts and required qualifications. There was an unexplained pay gap of 12%, which is attributable to discrimination. Another study conducted on hotels and restaurants in the Andalusia region of Spain found a pay gap of 7.9%–11.1%, caused mostly because of gender discrimination – both horizontal and vertical (Campos-Soria et al., 2009). To sum up, studies on the gender pay gap suggest that most of this is attributable to gender discrimination, on the basis of horizontal and vertical segregation, external labour mobility, and marital status.

Skalpe (2007) discovered a pay gap of 20% between male and female CEOs in the tourism industry in Norway, possibly because while there were more female CEOs in the hospitality industry, they were employed in relatively smaller firms. Bertrand and Hallock (2001) found major differences between the size of the companies in which men and women held top management positions; female senior managers tended to be working with much smaller corporations than their male counterparts. These results can be directly associated with the tendency for the salary of the CEO to increase with the size of the company. In another study conducted in Norway, Thrane (2008) also found a 20% pay gap in the tourism and hospitality industry as a whole. This study found that female employees benefit more from increased education levels in the form of wage premiums, as compared to men. On the other hand, male employees stand to gain from increased levels of work experience.

A study by Marfil Cotilla and Campos-Soria (2021) reaffirms the existence of the pay gap between men and women in the hospitality industry. This study, in the context of the Spanish hospitality industry, finds that 84.77% of the pay gap can be attributed to gender discrimination, with more men occupying higher paying positions and longer tenure. Women, on the other hand, are stuck in 'positions of low and medium responsibility' (p. 9), with the likelihood of comparatively lower pay increases at the time of promotion.

Another important finding from this study is the 'motherhood penalty', that is, female employees faced wage decreases of 8% for 'each additional child below the age of 11' (p. 520). The male employees, on the other hand, were offered a corresponding wage premium of 5%. The 'motherhood penalty' in terms of salary losses becomes more pronounced for highly skilled women (England et al., 2016). There are two reasons to account for this: (a) the necessary time off required to have children and (b) a possible reduction in the number of hours and flexible time options availed by female workers while shouldering childcare responsibilities (Dashper, 2019).

Purcell (1996) also points out that apart from differences in salaries/wages, men stand to gain from fringe benefits as well. This is because men in the hospitality industry are significantly more likely than women to obtain 'perks' such as 'company cars, free or subsidized meals, low-cost housing, private health insurance, company share ownership schemes and product discounts' (p. 22).

Other barriers: There may be other organizational barriers that may hamper women's career progression, in the form of discriminatory systems and processes that are often rooted in traditional gender roles and stereotypes. These barriers may be encountered anywhere in the course of women's work lives.

Dezsö et al. (2016) point out that while the presence of more women in boardrooms may be generally beneficial for increased female representation in senior management, firms may have implicit quotas in hiring. The senior management may, therefore, make minimal to no efforts, or in some cases even resist appointing more women to senior management teams or boards. In other words, the women already appointed are done to 'check a box', reducing them to token presences in senior management/boards.

Recruiters in the Portuguese hospitality industry tend to look for people who are 'flexible', that is, available for work even outside what is considered as normal working hours, known as 'availability-related flexibility' (Costa et al., 2017). Women are considered to be responsible for childcare and are thus often at a disadvantage when it comes to hiring decisions.

Studies have shown that women may not be offered critical, difficult assignments that are often linked with career advancement prospects (King et al., 2012), or they are evaluated against highly subjective measures. Women's efforts at self-improvement and career development are often hampered because they may not have timely access to information or performance feedback (Bear, Cushenbery, London, & Sherman, 2017). Studies from the hospitality industry also point out several organizational barriers. Karunarathna (2015) highlights the insufficient number of women in upper management and the subsequent lack of role models in the Sri Lankan context. Ng and Pine (2003) found a lack of support systems at work, a lack of equity in promotions, inadequate job knowledge, and a lack of mentoring/coaching as the major obstacles for women in Hong Kong. Li and Wang-Leung (2001), in a study conducted in Singapore, found that women were hampered by the 'old boys' network' with little or no access to informal networks. The authors contend that women may be unable to engage in networking, training, and other such activities critical for career advancement because of the long working hours and shifts. Finally, in a study conducted by Boone et al. (2013), participants mentioned the lack of mentoring and that of career planning and assignments as the main organizational barriers to women's career advancement.

Executive search bias? Executive search firms or 'headhunters' is often done by an external agency that matches critical leadership positions with candidates from high potential individuals for senior leadership positions. In a sense they act as 'gatekeepers' in that they are responsible for screening several profiles and then choosing what they think is suitable for the hiring client. However, research suggests that there are biases at this level too, which could prevent the profiles of high-performing women from being shortlisted. Often male headhunters believe that men are more competent and thus they don't try hard enough to identify female candidates (Siegel et al., 2020). Another study suggests that when there is a more male-dominated selection committee, fewer women make it into the hiring pool (Van den Brink et al., 2006).

Work–Life Interface

Traditional gendered division of labour is predicated upon the idea that home and work are separate, where men work outside the house, and women are engaged in running the household. The image of the 'ideal worker' is a derivative of this gendered division of labour, as someone who is engaged in labour outside the house for a set period of time, all year around, and who is supported by a stay-at-home spouse (Smith & Hatmaker, 2017). So while organizations have been posited as gender-neutral, in reality, the gendered nature of organizations and organizational processes does exist, specifically where the ideal worker is a man.

Blair-Loy (2003) identifies two schemas which are expressions of the ideal worker norm and the gendered division of labour. Work devotion, inherently masculine in nature, demands complete allegiance and commitment to work with a significant amount of time dedicated to working, whereas family devotion revolves around the assumption that women are in charge of the family, and that they find fulfilment and meaning in caregiving, with motherhood as their primary allegiance. Prior research emphasized that childcare was the primary barrier in a woman's career development, but eldercare has become a barrier too – one that is likely to gain more importance as the population ages (Morgan & Pritchard, 2018).

Often working women find it hard to reconcile these two roles. In fact, working women often report feeling guilty for not spending enough time with the family while working, and not prioritizing work while spending time with the family (Blair-Loy, 2003). There is also a stigma attached in drawing on company policies and strategies aimed at balancing work and family, with employers possibly assuming that the employee in question may be less committed to work (Leslie et al., 2012).

In such a context, women who seek career progression in the form of management positions may be required to stifle their desire for a work–life balance. In fact, in a work–life balance study, Doherty found that women in the hospitality industry were discouraged from seeking senior management roles because of the very long hours and the lack of flexibility. The study also confirms that 'a male model of a career based on commitment in the form of long hours persists' (Doherty, 2004, p. 448).

A counterview to the above studies was one conducted on C-suite executives employed with international companies across the tourism and hospitality industry by Boone et al. (2013). They found no significant difference between professional ambitions of the male and female participants. The significant finding from their study was that rather than the workplace imposing barriers, it was women's self-imposed barriers relating to their choices regarding family and household responsibilities, that held them back. They also suggest that these self-imposed barriers might be the result of leadership failures, rather than discriminatory practices.

Chapter 3

Study Results: Barriers to Woman Leadership in Hospitality Industry

Study Method

From the literature review, several antecedents to the phenomenon were examined including pay parity, unequal opportunities, the pipeline problem, and work–life interface. The study methodology for this exploratory study is as follows.

Primary research: To examine the antecedents of why there are so few women in leadership positions in the hospitality industry in India, 23 in-depth interviews were conducted of senior leaders and mid-level leaders, both male and female. The respondents were from several hotel groups in India including Le Meridian, The Leela Palaces, Hotels and Resorts, Intercontinental, Sarovar, Marriott, Crown Plaza, Sheraton, Radisson, Accor, OYO Hotels & Homes, Hotelivate, Wyndham, Lemon Tree, Taj, Fortune Park, and Hyatt Hotels Corporation. Designations included Managing Director, Senior Vice President, Country Head, General Manager, and Director of Human Resources (see Table 2). The work experience of the respondents ranged from 9 years to 40 years, with a mean average of 25 years.

Every interview was fully transcribed by a team of research associates (each interview ranging from 1,500 to 6,000 words). From these interviews, relevant codes and categories were drawn, leading to a compilation of personal narratives around the theme of women and equal opportunities (two coders were used in order to maintain accuracy and eliminate researcher bias). Within-case analysis was followed by between-case analysis, leading to second order themes (Miles & Huberman, 1994). Once the interviews were coded and within-case and

Table 2.   Sample Representation of Gender and Job Ranking.

	Male	Female
Senior	12	7
Mid-manager	1	3

Source: Author's own.

Gender Equity in Hospitality: The Case of India, 25–40
Copyright © 2023 by Payal Kumar
Published under exclusive licence by Emerald Publishing Limited
doi:10.1108/978-1-80382-665-320231003

between-case themes elicited, a thematic tree of first and second order concepts was created (see Fig. 2).

Secondary data collection: Some data on gender representation in the work-place were collected on the representation of woman leaders in luxury hotels, as no such consolidated data exist at present (see Appendix Table A2).

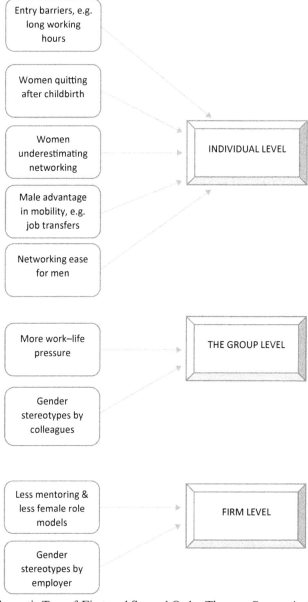

Fig. 2.   Thematic Tree of First and Second Order Themes. *Source*: Author's own.

Post-study round-table discussion: Post the qualitative interviews, a focus group discussion was held among woman leaders from a variety of other industries, to gauge whether the results of this study were specific to the hospitality industry or more generalizable.

Themes Elicited from Interviews

Some of the barriers that emerged from this study are:

(i)   Lack of pay parity.
(ii) Unequal opportunities/training.
(iii) Pipeline problem.
(iv) Lack of safety.
(v)   Stereotypical views of employers and male co-workers.
(vi) Work–life interface: managing household (dual role).

In more detail, here are the common themes that have emerged from the multiple interviews,[1] leading to a thematic tree (see below).

1. Entry barriers:
A 'leaky pipeline' is a metaphor for underrepresentation of women at various stages of career progression, for example, at the entry level there are not enough women joining the workforce in the first place (due to entry barriers), thus leading to fewer women being in the pool of candidates for possible promotion to leadership roles.

- 'Long operational work hours are a discouragement for women in the industry because it comes in conflict with their family obligations.' (R8-M-F)
- 'There is a lot of social stigma in the conservative society that we all live in, for women to serve alcohol and tobacco products.' (R23-M-M)
- 'Women are more susceptible to harassment, not only inside, but outside the organization.' (R7-M-F)
- 'You know in that especially in hotels, very few girl would do night shifts. Because if you force them to night shifts, parents won't allow.' (R6-S-M)
- 'I have been told that government officials have to be met in the hospitality sector, and that government officials are not very comfortable with women around.' (R5-S-F)
- 'There is also this bias that we have in India that society looks down upon on the females who are working in hotels with odd timings.' (R18-S-F)

---

[1]Interviewee names are anonymous. Direct quotations are represented by a code: respondent number–senior/mid-manager–male/female.

- 'The job often demands large amounts of time and physical presence/work: sometimes up to 14 hours, commitment to job (it's demanding physically and time-wise).' (R7-M-F)
- 'Unfortunately I have seen organizations who are more eager to hire male employees and you've seen that and it's a mindset.' (R14-S-M)

Mr Manav Thadani, Founder Chairman at Hotelivate

Unfortunately we still live in a very male-dominated society. So while there's a lot of lip service I think because of the work hours and late nights it becomes more difficult for women to kind of be available during the longer periods. If they're an average hotel person starting off in the hotel industry, they may not necessarily have the 40 hours work week, right. At a manager level, you could be looking at 60–70 hours of work. I think it kind of pushes women away from the hotel sector because these are not nine to five jobs. I think that is the biggest barrier.

So we do see women in the hospitality sector, a lot of them in the HR and marketing, because that again can be a little bit more structured by the nine to five jobs and at the operation level very few because of the crazy working hours. As an industry, we need to come up with a lot more flexibility in the hours. And I don't know whether this problem is an individual company level or is it governed by the local authorities but I would rather see people being allowed to do like half day work or even doing one and a half days at a time because I think it just provide more flexibility not just to women employees but also generally to all employees.

---

2. *Quitting/taking a break after childbirth:*
   Studies suggest that if a woman takes even a short break from work due to childbirth, childcare or for care of the elderly, she is never able to catch up in the career growth compared to her male counterparts (Cools, Markussen, & Strøm, 2017). To do away with this 'motherhood penalty' countries such as Norway ensure that returning mothers rejoin in the same position as men even after a career break, thus balancing the scales.

- 'Many of our woman colleagues leave after getting married or after having a child – then there's a gap in the career and it's difficult to make up for those lost years. This often depletes the talent pool.' (R10-S-M)
- 'I remember when I was a general manager the organization tried a lot of new policies, and we did get a lot of women, but then if they would have children they would leave.' (R12-S-F)
- 'So in the hospitality industry because of long hours what happens is that once they're married they want to have children, which becomes a challenge for them.' (R12-S-F)
- 'Will you be able to travel with kids, manage different demands and schedules if pregnant? It's a question worth asking.' (R7-M-F)

- 'Long operational work hours are a discouragement for women to continue in the industry because it comes into conflict with their family obligations.' (R8-M-F)
- 'It could be that maybe women have entered into family responsibilities, maybe had their first child, second child, and are going through a difficult personal life responsibilities.' (R22-S-F)
- 'We also have cases where a female candidate have to leave her job to take care of the family as soon as she got married.' (R18-S-F)

Mr Sunjae Sharma, Managing Director – India and Southwest Asia at Hyatt Hotels Corporation

Despite consistent evidence proving the connection between diverse and inclusive workplaces and profitability and performance, the industry has been mostly unsuccessful in levelling the gender equity playing field. Building a gender-inclusive workplace doesn't just mean hiring more women and better pay equity. While this is certainly a good first step, gender inequity is a deeply rooted systemic issue, and therefore requires work at the foundational level.

A truly inclusive work culture ensures that every employee, regardless of their gender identity, feels supported, cared for, and respected. In addition to this sense of belonging, a work culture focussed on gender inclusion has the power to elevate previously unheard voices and value diverse experiences, fostering an environment of authentic respect and trust.

---

3. *Less female mobility to job locations:*
   It is striking that in the hospitality industry, possibly more than other industries, geographical mobility seems to be a pre-requisite for upward career growth. Often managers are sent out to different locations not only in the country, but to establishments abroad too. Family responsibilities, such as wanting a fixed school location for the children, often deters women from moving to different locations on a constant basis, thus impeding their growth.

- 'When you have a family and children, it becomes it becomes difficult for them to kind of uproot themselves and go to another location.' (R9-M-F)
- 'The biggest barrier that I have seen preventing women from rising is mobility. It is not easy to stay at the same location for a long time and keep growing.' (R2-S-M)
- 'In case of women employees, mobility becomes a barrier due to reasons such as personal commitments, having young children, as well as the way our societies are structured which put an uneven share of domestic responsibilities on women.' (R2-S-M)
- 'So she can't go though it's a great job in Bombay because the husband is in Delhi. Whereas if the husband got a job in Bombay then she would have to leave a job in Delhi and go to Bombay with him.' (R11-S-M)
- 'They'll say I cannot go there or my husband is posted in Delhi. I have to stay in Delhi only or my children are going to school. I have to stay here only.' (R21-S-M)

- 'If they're on a transferable job, then it becomes absolutely impossible … how many women will want to separate themselves from their family and go live in another city?' (R9-M-F)
- 'Then you have logistical issues, right. Like the child is somewhere, then the husband is working then you need family support. So those without family support they cannot climb the ladder.' (R9-M-F)
- 'The male generally says fine I don't mind if from Delhi you're posting me to Chennai. I will go. I will find the place in case no accommodation is given. For a lady, unless there's accommodation given she will not go, she is not likely to go.' (R21-S-M)

Mr Anuraag Bhatnagar, Chief Operating Officer, Leela Palaces, Hotels & Resorts

The biggest barrier that I have seen preventing women from rising is mobility. At Leela we have presence in over 14 cities. It is not easy to stay at the same location for a long time and keep growing. In order to grow vertically you need to move horizontally. One needs to change work locations geographically and move between different zones and regions. In case of women employees, mobility becomes a barrier due to reasons such as personal commitments, having young children as well as the way our societies are structured which put an uneven share of domestic responsibilities on women.

For example, we have a case of a very seasoned and experienced woman Hotel Manager in Delhi who is being offered General Manger position at a different location. So, while a promotion opening exists for her in the next three months in a different location, the same position may not be available to her in Delhi due to a different incumbent continuing for next three years. This is a real challenge posed by our business being spread across locations.

The second major challenge is maintaining a healthy work–life balance. Hospitality demands real presence on the site and long working hours. There are limits to work from home type arrangements in hospitality. There are no fixed working hours and unlike other sectors, business peaks during weekends, holidays, and vacations. So, the very nature of business expects us to sacrifice and forgo many of our personal special occasions in order to serve our guests.

I have myself seen good women employees missing out on opportunities due to mobility and work–life issues. On numerous occasions, I have spoken to such women associates and ensured that we can be as flexible as possible. We try our best to offer positions that are closer to their home bases.

We help them with work–life balance by offering shifts, off days, adequate and special leaves. We try our best to mitigate and work around these challenges, by offering work from home, flexible working hours and other accommodations; still the geographical mobility remains a challenge. The reality is that ours is not a hands off job. A hotel cannot have two General Managers. A hotelier is supposed to be in the hotel and cannot effectively function remotely through camera. It is unfortunate that several women employees relinquish key positions because their family is not supportive of their moving to a different city. Family support is crucial to a woman's career growth.

4. *Women underestimating the power of networking:*
Research suggests that often women do not realize the power of networking and thus may give this less credence, which in turn means that they may lose out in certain ways, such as being exposed to fewer opportunities available at the senior level. Mark Granovetter's (1973) well-known study on 'The strength of weak ties' shows that even second and third tier network nodes can prove to be effective in a job search.

- 'Expanding your contacts can open doors to new opportunities for business, career advancement, personal growth, or simply new knowledge.' (R10-S-M)
- 'It's very important and I think sometimes women underestimate the power of networking and there is a very valid reason for that because we are embroiled in our personal life a little more than men, we feel ourselves personally responsible for family matters and thus we are compelled to look after home, children as well along with our professional careers.' (R22-S-F)
- 'Today with leaders if you want to grow in the ranks and you want to grow up, you have to be able to influence people, it's not about sitting in a corner and doing a good job and by yourself, you have to be able to influence people.' (R12-S-F)
- 'Networking is particularly important at senior leadership level where the expectation is for a person to be well recognized and respect industry leader.' (R2-S-M)
- 'Active networking helps to keep you top of mind when opportunities such as job openings arise and increases your likelihood of receiving introductions to potentially relevant people or even a referral.' (R10-S-M)
- 'Many jobs don't even get advertised – particularly as your career advances – so being a recognized part of networks is a keyway to gain access to opportunities that you might not have otherwise.' (R10-S-M)

Ms Monisha Dewan, Senior Area Director, Sales and Distribution, South Asia at Marriott International

Mentoring and networking is super important because today with leaders if you want to grow in the ranks and you want to grow up, you have to be able to influence people, it's not about sitting in a corner and doing a good job and by yourself, you have to be able to influence people. If you have to be able to influence people, you need to be able to network. You need to be visible. People need to be able to see.

If there's a young woman who comes in and she's looking at this, she's wondering, how do I get that presence? How do I develop that gravitas? How do I get the world to see me? She needs help. She needs mentorship, someone to tell her the rules, someone to explain things to her. And it's easier for a man than a woman to network. So an informal mentoring, networking structure needs to be created, it is very important.

My biggest advice for any woman who enters a leadership position is that she has to be very authentic, be herself, not try to change who she is. The fact that she's reached where she has reached means that she has done something very good.

5. *Ease of forming mentorship networks for men*:
It's the usual story that has been playing out for a few generations: the female employee tends to rush home to care for her family, while her male counterpart may go out for a drink or stay on at the workplace for longer hours to perhaps attend a workplace function or social gathering – and thus get ahead in networking.

- 'Mentorship plays a huge role in promotion and selection for one's next role. This may be easier for male employees to procure.' (R2-S-M)
- 'Mentorship also becomes crucial when a professional is learning and preparing to go up the ladder in that case it becomes very important.' (R23-M-M)
- 'And you know in the corporate there is an old boys' club. They go drinking and socialise after work.' (R5-S-F)
- 'Another problem that women have is that women do not have the same kind of networking privileges a man has.' (R12-S-F)
- 'If there are too many men, especially at the top and you're reporting to men and you're surrounded by men ... as women, we like to have a few more of our kind.' (R9-M-F)
- 'So you are at a disadvantage in terms of networking because maybe your male colleague have a better chance at it.' (R9-M-F)

- 'Often men don't prefer to network with women as they look upon them with either sympathy, or they will not understand their problems because they've not been in their shoes.' (R12-S-F)
- 'There are more than enough role models of men running around the world, but there are very limited role models for women.' (R12-S-F)
- 'The industry can collaborate more on mentorship. Woman leaders should be provided mentoring for taking up larger roles.' (R15-S-M)

6. *Work–life pressure challenges for women:*
   Double pressure of work and family responsibilities is one of the main reasons that so many women are dropping out of the workforce in India. Those who do continue working often suffer from the guilt of spending time at work rather than being with young children or ailing, elderly members at home.

- 'I think top barriers for women is lack of family support.' (R9-M-F)
- 'At the end of the day it is a fact that in India, women have to go back and do much more at home than a man does.' (R5-S-F)
- 'It is fact, the primary responsibility of food or the kids ends up on the woman's lap. And that overwhelms women because if you are working 8–10 hours a day and travel you have so much to do.' (R5-S-F)
- 'A second reason relates to a lot of women dropping out at the mid-management level to give more time to their families.' (R1-S-F)
- 'If she is already married then she has to take care of the family as well. So all of this result in her choosing to leave her job rather than to continue with the pressure of juggling both the jobs at the same time.' (R18-S-F)

Ms Kanika Hasrat, Area Director UP, MP, and Uttarakhand and General Manager at Taj Lakefront Bhopal at The Indian Hotel Company Limited

I believe that a lot of times choosing between family and a career becomes a problem for women. As the very time the career graph rises, women are also at their prime to start a family, and so setting priorities is tough. In India, the mother is considered the primary caregiver and that is non-negotiable in most homes. Working 9 hours and then going back home to take care of the kids and the family brings a different sets of challenges. This I believe is perhaps the biggest barrier that a woman faces to grow in her career and is not specific only to the hospitality industry. Should she get through those vital years with the help of her family and organization – she is set for success.

7. *Gender stereotypes by colleagues:*
In patriarchal societies, male colleagues may not think women to be as capable or willing to put in hard work. Even fewer would accept a woman as their boss.

- 'Not every male can accept a female boss so I think that we have to remove the bias and work only on the basis of merit.' (R4-S-M)
- 'If you see the HR heads of all the hotels in India are all females, barring few. Most of them are all ladies.' (R6-S-M)
- 'Maybe sometimes when the leadership changes, the dynamics can change. If the top manager is a male, he might not be very comfortable with women – there are people like that.' (R9-M-F)
- 'If you pull the data, a majority of leadership roles are men. So in changing or removing these barriers, it is an issue of sensitizing leaders to sensitize male employees, and you can do this by then looking at those women who have reached a leadership positions.' (R11- S-M)
- 'Occasionally we still have discussions when people say that they don't want a woman GM at their property.' (R3-S-M)
- 'I would say that most of the men are a little sexist.' (R6-S-M)
- 'I think part of it is, unfortunately, that we still live in a very male dominated society.' (R14-S-M)
- 'Unfortunately, while most customers are decent, sometimes colleagues may not be that decent. So then one has to have those policies in place to see harassment at work, doesn't take place.' (R21-S-M)
- 'Men will cover up for men, even at the cost of a woman colleague, and give benefit of doubt to male colleagues.' (R7-M-F)

Mr Sudeep Jain, Managing Director, South West Asia at InterContinental Hotels Group

I don't think that the situation is that bad today. Yes we are still lagging behind when we see the West, but we are getting there slowly and gradually. Right, occasionally we still have discussions when people say that they don't want a woman GM at their property. I am not saying that you don't hear that, we do. But, what the situation might have been 10 years back it has certainly improved today. So you talk to both men and women and try to understand where we are and how we can improve the situation. And keep improving it continuously.

Having said that there are also cases where we see women making a choice not to go up the hierarchy for various reasons – usually we listen from them is about taking care of their families and hours not being very flexible. And we have to work on these gaps that exists to make it more accessible. Also, because we have a male dominated industry the percentage of job application that we get is heavily skewed towards men. We see a glaring difference between men applying for the same job.

Some of the respondents spoke of at times men feeling discriminated against in the face of pro-women policies, such as hotels providing a night drop vehicle to women (as per legal requirements).

- 'At a bigger hotel you cannot differentiate much between the genders because the boys will say that there is a discrimination happening. Please understand from their (boys) point of view. They will also start saying that there is a discrimination.' (R6-S-M)
- 'Often men have to do the more laborious work in the kitchen. For kitchen work – not many girls are opting for kitchen.' (R6-S-M)

There are divergent opinions on human resource departments often being headed by women. Some see this as a sign of them 'taking up a soft option', while others are of the view that this is in fact progressive.

- 'It helps to have a very strong leading HR Director who happens to be a woman herself and understands the needs of employees.' (R8-M-F)

8. *Gender stereotypes by organizations:*
   'Think manager, think male' is a common refrain (Schein & Davidson, 1993), and so is the paternalistic tendency of some organizations.

- 'Unfortunately I have seen organizations who are more eager to hire male employees and you've seen that and it's a mindset.' (R14-S-M)
- 'I have had owner telling me that we do not want women GM.' (R5-S-F)
- 'Often we are "not believed" by HR when certain wrongs which were happening was reported, even though it was found to be true later, e.g. sexist comments.' (R9-M-F)
- 'Industry needs to be more supportive and collaborative and not have any bias against women. There is need for a change of mindset so as to promote women leadership.' (R15-S-M)
- 'For instance, over there was not a single lady GM in the resort, maybe because they are all in remote locations and maybe they feel a lady cannot handle the responsibility.' (R9-M-F)
- 'Expectation from ladies is to be soft. So if you are in human resources you should be soft, not loud, not regimental.' (R7-M-F)
- 'If we critically analyze our workplace infrastructure, dress and uniforms, aesthetics, processes, etc. we will find several hidden biases in things such as seating, uniforms, designs, etc.' (R1-S-F)
- 'If there is a very important position and they feel that this woman has just got married they may not hire her only because they assume she will soon take maternity leave. That's the mindset she's fighting.' (R12-S-F)
- 'Perception of the leaders of the industry or of companies in being able to instill that responsibility amongst women leaders, there is probably a slight hesitation.' (R22-S-F)

Ms Aradhana Lal, Vice President-Brand, Communications and Sustainability Initiatives at Lemon Tree Hotels

For us it doesn't matter whether it is a man or a woman. It doesn't matter whether it's a person with a disability or without disability. It doesn't matter whether it's a person from an economically and socially marginalized background or not – to us, they are all possible candidates on account of our equal opportunity policy. Then if we give them the right inputs and training, if they have a positive attitude and strong desire to learn, we are able to mainstream them at our hotels and help them grow. In fact, it is our dream to one day have a Hotel General Manager who is a person with a disability. We haven't got there yet, but the dream is alive and we are working on it.

9. *Less role models for women:*
   Research shows that role modelling has a positive impact in career progression. But do women have enough role models to learn from?

   - 'It's not always possible for the new entrants to get trained. You also observe and learn from what your seniors are doing in a given situation.' (R4-S-M)
   - 'Because of the fact that we lack woman leaders, when women see other women as leaders, they naturally say right, if she can make it so can I.' (R11-S-M)
   - 'So that's an area we are trying to focus on, how to create more lady hotel managers. At the moment this number is very, very less, but there are two of them who are very much in the making.' (R17-S-F)
   - 'There are fewer women leaders out there and when we look at the industry we have very few woman general managers, and also very few property owners. You can name a few but that's about it.' (R14-S-M)
   - 'But it should not be a man coaching a woman on diversity as he will not understand the problems that she's facing.' (R12-S-F)
   - 'There are more than enough role models of men running around the world but there are very limited women.' (R12-S-F)
   - 'If we have more women in the industry then it is a lot easier for others to watch them and get inspired.' (R23-M-M)

10. *Lack of facilities for women:*

    - 'Infrastructure needs to be reassessed by some sort of a certification body to see that the processes, infrastructure, the office, the hotel, the product is compliant with the expectations of a woman.' (R22-S-F)
    - 'Lack of transportation and security support for women is apparent.' (R7-M-F)
    - 'There were no woman-centric HR policies. They were not for nor against, but they there was nothing to ensure that you would be retained.' (R9-M-F)

- 'So what leadership can do is create a framework for sensitization of breaking these barriers, in order for women to grow into leadership, for example, by breaking up those familial issues which come up.' (R11-S-M)
- 'Maybe in hotels we need to have a crèche so that women who take up long hours or second shifts can do so in spite of familial responsibilities.' (R22-S-F)
- 'It's all things like having a sanitary, napkin dispenser in all public washroom in case of any sort of emergency – how difficult is that for something like that to be institutionalized?' (R22-S-F)
- 'The budgets are small and thus small hotels cannot provide night shifts drop because in night shifts you have to provide both a guard and a chauffeur.' (R6-S-M)

Chef-turned-educator, Dr Zubin D'Souza, Dean for Culinary and Practical Arts, Indian School of Hospitality

Personally, I have seen a slew of extremely successful young ladies in the hotel industry. I think that the industry has evolved and matured in the terms of gender balancing over the last three decades. There are two sides to this issue and both are rather pertinent. Unfortunately, the Indian mindset of a working lady needs her to balance work with the needs of the family. Consequently, they look for an assignment that allows them to balance the rigours of the work in the hotel industry with the varied shifts and their family life. They either tend to choose comparatively easier sections like Sales, Marketing, HR where the work hours are fixed, or they move out of the industry altogether. If they do choose departments with fixed working hours, the opportunities to rise become comparatively limited because the number of vacancies or possible movement opportunities drop dramatically. Honestly, the hotel industry needs to be regulated for the draconian work timings that everyone is expected to adhere to. This is an unofficial expectation because on paper the associates seem to be working according to nationally stipulated norms. I definitely feel that making a hotel supportive to new parents could be a great start. Also taking constructive feedback on a regular basis and implementing these ideas would be great.

Based on the interviews, a thematic tree of first and second order concepts was created (see Fig. 2).

Post-study Round-table Discussion

Post the qualitative interviews, a focus group discussion was held in Gurgaon, India, on 5 May 2022. Women leaders from a variety of industries (e.g. media, publishing, academia, and entrepreneurship) were invited for a discussion on gender equity and leadership, in order to gauge whether the results of this study were specific to the hospitality industry in general, or were common across industries. The enthusiastic discussion, scheduled for two hours, went on for an hour longer than expected.

A few questions were put forward by me as the lead to the group in order to start the discussion, with an aim to have a free-flowing discussion to elicit several themes (rather than pre-empting themes through a structured format of questioning). Some of the questions were:

- What about other industries? Why is it that women seem to excel in some industries at the leadership level in India such as banking, and yet not in others?
- Why do thousands of qualified women give up working after childbirth, comparatively more than in other countries?
- For those that do re-enter the formal workforce, is there a 'maternal wall' wherein employers assume that family priorities take precedence over work deliverables? Why is it that women who return to the workplace after a break are often never able to play 'catch-up' with their male colleagues in terms of career progression?
- What other challenges do women face in terms of career progression?

The themes elicited from this discussion can be classified into and 'barriers and enablers' for leadership.

Barriers

Female-to-Female Friction

Participant: Monisha Chowla, Operations Director, Media Monks, India
While taking us through her professional journey, Monisha spoke about the contrast between male and female employers. When she began her career with NDTV 20 years ago, there were more women than men at the organization. She said, 'While woman managers were supportive and empathetic, they would also become insecure when another woman in the team performs better. I have observed that their insecurities come out'.

Women Can Be Patriarchal Too

Participant: Sangeeta Menon, Publishing Relationship Manager, Emerald Publishing
Sangeeta began her career as a journalist 20 years ago and then turned to editing and publishing later on. She spoke about the challenges that younger generation of women face and says she enjoys helping them tackle these challenges as a mentor. She says, 'The patriarchal burden that women carry is tremendous. As a society we need to realize that women can be patriarchal as well and that changing mindsets will take time'.

Bias Against Working Mothers Is Real

Participant: Tanuja Sharma, Professor & LEAD Centre for Ethics, ESG and Responsible Organizations, MDI, Gurgaon

Tanuja Sharma has over 30 years of experience in academia. When asked about the advice she would give to her 20-year-old self, Professor Tanuja spoke about the importance of being yourself and comfortable in your own skin. She went on to mention her experience of interviewing women on maternity leave for her research work and said,

> The bias against women because of their duties as a mother are glaring. We need to move beyond the rights and responsibilities society has set for us and think more independently. Returning mothers should be honoured, not victimised. We also need to alter myths. For example, why do we have to perform all the time? Why can't we instead focus on being competent and on being our authentic self.

Enablers

Moving Out of the Comfort Zone

Participant: Anindita Moitra, doctoral scholar
Anindita is doing her doctoral on: 'Representation of Women Directors in Boardrooms and their Contribution towards Corporate Governance'. She began her career as a chemical engineer more than 30 years ago. As one of the few women in a typically male-dominated industry, she faced numerous setbacks along the way, for example, she was told that the most she could aspire to be was a typist. Through grit and perseverance, she took on these challenges and rose to many prominent positions in her field. While talking about the lack of equality in the workplace, Anindita pointed out that women need to come together if they want to break the glass ceiling.

> Family and societal support is very necessary for women to succeed in any profession. At the same time, women with high qualifications shouldn't choose a life of comfort by just sticking to female-dominated sectors.

Supportive Supervisor

Participant: Smita Mishra, Founder and CEO, Fandoro Technologies Pvt. Ltd.
With more than 20 years of experience as a software engineer, Smita now heads Fandoro, a SaaS platform that helps companies achieve sustainability. Fandoro was recently awarded the 'Start-up of the Year' by the Government of India. Smita spoke about how a supportive supervisor allowed her to achieve her professional goals. She says,

> When I was working for an MNC as an expectant mother, my female supervisor took great care of me. She would take me out

for short walks, and even gave me something to elevate my feet with in order to prevent ankle swelling. Furthermore, allowing for flexi-timings when I joined back as a new mother was tremendously useful in supporting me to continue to work and not extend my leave or quit working.

Working on an Equal Footing with Men

Participant: Sangeeta Thakur, Consultant – Content, Communications, and Media; Managing Editor, 9.9 Editor
Having worked as a content, communications, and media specialist all her career, Sangeeta spoke about the support she received from her male colleagues and superiors throughout her life. Sangeeta mentioned that, 'The fact that we are struggling with issues of gender equity after all these years is in itself a disgrace'. She feels that, 'In order to be empowered, women need to push themselves forward and ask for things they feel they truly deserve'. She gives her own example, when she was asked to work in the night shift of a reputed newspaper office, shoulder-to-shoulder with her male colleagues.

Having the Courage to Take Charge

Participant: Dr Jaskiran Arora, Dean and Head of Centre for Teaching and Learning, BML Munjal University
Jaskiran Arora speaks about how women need to be more assertive to be able to make a space for themselves in their field. She recalls that as a girl she had once slapped a boy who was harassing her while she was walking on a road. She says that incident gave her courage to take things in her own hands when required. Today, as Dean she plays a role in both mentoring female students and faculty, while also role modelling for them.

Chapter 4

Models for Individual and Systematic Change

Firm-level Examples

The topic of gender equity in the hospitality industry in India is not all one of doom and gloom. There are some exciting initiatives at the firm level and also inspirational success stories at the individual level, some of which are represented in this chapter.

In fact, Ritu Verma, Senior Vice President Human Resources, India and Middle, Brookfield Asset Management, goes so far as to say that this is a great time for women today.

> When I started about 24 years ago, it was a different world. But now organizations really want diversity. They want the diversity not just on the agenda, but they want to diversify their boards. I think it's a great time for women and I think that they should make the best of it.

Take Hyatt Hotels Corporation, which often ranks high in Fortune's best workplaces for women. One of their initiatives is placing all women at entry level into a specially curated networking programme known as 'Inspirit', which aims to support their leadership aspirations, while meeting the company's aspiration to foster an inclusive workplace. Similarly, Intercontinental Hotel has a programme called 'Riise', which is targeted at mid-management level woman candidates, providing them with a mentoring circle and formalized mentoring and training. At The Indian Hotels Company Limited too there is a programme known as 'One-to-One' mentorship programme, where a female candidate can choose any female or male senior leader to be her guide.

With a current diversity mix at The Leela Palaces, Hotels, and Resorts at above 27%, the group is striving to take gender diversity to at least 30%. There is a well-structured executive development plan in place for grooming future leaders which includes a strength-and-needs analysis of individual associates, buddy

Gender Equity in Hospitality: The Case of India, 41–48
Copyright © 2023 by Payal Kumar
Published under exclusive licence by Emerald Publishing Limited
doi:10.1108/978-1-80382-665-320231004

and mentor assignments, counselling and coaching facility, and also a practice of shadowing a leader. Women associates are also offered special leaves and flexible working hours.

Wyndham Hotels and Resorts has a female representation ranging between 25% and 40% at the senior management level globally and in India. At the executive level, 100% gender pay equity has been achieved. Furthermore, human trafficking awareness training has been mandated across hotels and corporate team members.

Then there is Lemon Tree Hotels which defines 'diversity and inclusion' quite widely, not just limited to gender. In fact, its policies are geared to mainstream 'opportunity deprived individuals (ODIs)'. This consists of two sub segments, employees with disability and employees from economically and socially marginalized backgrounds. Hiring includes candidates that are deaf, have a physical handicap, are visually impaired, or have an intellectual/developmental disability like Down Syndrome or Autism. There is also a hiring drive on for acid survivors, transgenders, women who are economically and socially marginalized such as widows, divorcees, abandoned women, and orphans/abandoned girls. In fact, about 10%–15% of the employee bases are ODIs, while women constitute approximately 9%–10%.

An Individual-level Example

Navigating her way from a housekeeping management trainee to General Manager of an ITC Hotel in Bangalore, one of India's leading metropolitan cities, is no mean feat. Amandeep Kaur's inspirational story (in an interview format with the author) is worth reading.

Give me a little background to yourself: How did you come into the hospitality industry?
Born in North India, New Delhi was a base for me in my school days. While I was a science student, I had aspirations to become a doctor. I guess from the very beginning I wanted to do something that resonated with my nature of wanting to serve. It was my father who recommended hotel management as a viable career option. This was rather uncharted territory and I didn't know much about the course. However, I passed the entrance exam of an Institute of Hotel Management and began my studies. In my final year, many hotel chains and hospitality-related firms visited the college for campus interviews. I was fortunate enough to receive several job opportunities. Looking back, today I can say with great pride that I took the right decision in joining ITC Hotels for their management training programme.

Please describe your career growth.
In 2005, once I had completed my management trainee tenure, I got my first posting at ITC Grand Central Hotel as Assistant Housekeeping Manager. From there, ITC gave me tremendous opportunities to work across lengths and breadths of India. Here are the positions I have held (in reverse chronological order):

- General Manager, Welcomhotel, Bengaluru, 2021–till date.
- Resident Manager, ITC Gardenia, Bengaluru, 2020–2021.
- Executive Housekeeper, ITC Gardenia, Bengaluru, 2019–2020.
- Executive Housekeeper, ITC, Grand Bharat, Delhi, 2016–2019.
- Assistant Executive Housekeeper, ITC Maratha, Mumbai, 2014–2016.
- Assistant Executive Housekeeper, ITC Grand Chola, Chennai, 2012–2014.
- Housekeeping Manager, Sheraton, 2008–2012.
- Housekeeping Manager, ITC Grand Central, Mumbai; ITC Gardenia, Bengaluru; ITC Sonar, Kolkata, 2005–2008.

What were the challenges and opportunities you faced as a fresher?
The ITC ecosystem fosters growth and at the same time provides enough tools and encouragement for everyone across all diverse backgrounds. I would say the journey has all been about opportunities, rather than challenges. The management institute's well-structured training programme armoured us with knowledge and enough shop floor exposure for us to take up our first posting with a lot of confidence. The diverse and very inclusive environment, along with continuous mentorship, provided us with a great platform to kick-start the new role. On a personal front, in the beginning, I must admit that I was a bit subdued and was a little hesitant to make friends initially. However, the work environment along with the accommodation provided by the organization, made this transition effortless. I ended up making great friends, and looking back have many lovely memories.

Could you name the factors which you think led to your success?
Whatever I have done in life has been driven by lot of passion and integrity, backed by a great set of mentors within the organization and outside as well. At ITC, at every stage of my career, I have been fortunate enough to have had some mentors, some inspiration to look up to and guide me through the process, which is a true reflection of the organization's great work culture. Personally, once I had made up my mind on the career path I wanted, I never limited myself to any one function or one particular job description that I was assigned to do. While my endeavour was always to excel in what I had been assigned, I would never be satisfied by doing just that. I have always seized opportunities to contribute at whatever time, and thankfully have never been discouraged by anyone. There was never a moment of discouragement.

On a personal front, there has been immense support and backing of my parents, who had no idea whatsoever what hotel management was really about. There's no one in the family who is remotely from this field. Yet, my parents were good enough to gauge that my intellect and interests were in tune with this industry. Now looking back at it I believe it was very courageous of my parents to take the decision to send me away from home to study something not commonly understood at that time, considering the middle class background they come from. I can't thank them enough. From parents, to my husband, in-laws, and now a child who has given me relentless support and backing to accelerate my career growth.

In your opinion, what are the barriers to the growth of women leaders in the industry? In other words, why are there so few women leaders in the hospitality sector in India?
It is unfortunate that there are very few women leaders in the hospitality sector. However, over the years there has been slow but a steady change in this trend, as well as in mindsets. Multitasking, decision-making, and handling various life situations efficiently, come naturally to women, and at the workplace, these really help you be your natural self.

That our industry requires 24×7 commitment is a myth. People believe that there is no sanctity of work–life balance in a hotelier's life. I believe work–life balance is person specific and not dependent on the industry one is working in. Also, while hard work is indispensable for any industry, irrespective of gender, other diverse factors are required to excel.

As a woman, I know that I am very fortunate to have the support of family members, my mentors, and my organization's humane and flexible policies, all of which helped me achieve my goals. However, in India, I do believe that there is still a large section of society where equality and shared responsibility are still very theoretical. In such scenarios, I do believe women face challenges, due to the absence of support and empathy. Women tend to work harder to prove their self-worth or earn an equal place at work, along with ensuring that personal responsibilities are not compromised.

Traditionally, man is the breadwinner and woman supports this endeavour. Likewise, now when women are working too, they also need strong support and backing to focus on their professional goals. The biological clock that everyone talks about is for real and it does coincide with the career trajectory. The absence of strong support and understanding from the family, and weak organization policies, can make it challenging for women wanting to pursue their careers.

Organizations such as ITC and many others are setting great examples, fostering a culture of equality, inclusion, and also providing that humane understanding in the form of flexible policies that assist women in managing hurdles better. Organizations such as these set the right example and are slowly assisting the country towards a more progressive approach which is not gender biased.

At times, it is external factors which make it hard for women to grow, or at times an internal battle that becomes an impediment to women's growth, Nature, I think has given a lot more EQ to women along with IQ, and hence sometimes they become too hard on themselves. As we are progressing and more women leaders are emerging in various industries, I do strongly believe that things are evolving, and that instead of discussions around gender differentiation, the focus will naturally shift towards collective thinking, collaboration, and shared goals irrespective of any gender, caste, creed etc. This shift can already be seen making a paradigm shift.

What words of encouragement would you give to young women entering the industry?
The first step is to acknowledge your self-worth, stop doubting yourself based on gender, and do not be too hard upon yourself. There is no shortcut to hard work, irrespective of gender and industry. Hard work is a misunderstood word I

feel; it doesn't always attribute to how much force is applied physically or number of hours one can stand on his/her feet to work. Rather hard work is a subjective matter where, while acquiring industry-based knowledge, one continues to invest in herself by pushing one's boundaries, learning beyond one's subject, creating a large knowledge archive for oneself, reading about diverse topics on related and non-related subjects, travel extensively, groom yourself well, and with every opportunity prepare well to give it the best shot every time. Focus on doing any small deed that'll inspire someone, and continue to grow and expand your knowledge horizon. Mentors play a major role in progress, hence never negate the power of good mentorship.

I also believe in maintaining a positive mindset, good communication, and also garnering support from family members. Your own confidence will attract a lot of supporters. Hotels are one of the most integrated yet diverse industries, with umpteen platforms available to help you develop yourself on personal grooming, communication, and business acumen, while providing you with opportunities to grow in various diverse functions. For example, thanks to ITC's aggressive talent development strategy and a strong belief in creating opportunities to groom the right capabilities, I have managed to transition from the function of housekeeping to general administration, and today am handling a unit independently. There are great career opportunities and with the industry booming back after COVID, it will further grow by leaps and bounds. One just needs the passion and vision for oneself, with undeterred determination. The industry will surely back all the young aspirants for them to achieve their dreams and career goals.

Please share in detail about good mentoring or training that you received.
ITC has always been very strong with its values and ethos towards talent management and growth opportunities and has structured its programme with the right mix of classroom learning, projects, and shop floor training for every level to grow to the next level. At every given phase of my career, I have been blessed and have been fortunate enough to have had great mentors who have given me the right inputs at the right time. Theoretically, yes, but there were more on-the-shop floor learning opportunities that instilled strong empowerment.

Looking back at my transition to general administration from a function-specific role, I realize I could adapt and learn faster because my mentor had me included in all aspects of general administration and overall operations right from day one of my training. With careful listening, observations, and participation, I was able to reach the next level of growth where I could make informed decisions. And slowly without realizing it, I started taking care of day-to-day operations, while making strategic decisions with ease for the hotel overall. I must admit that I embarrassed myself sometimes during this phase. However, my mentors told me that these professional struggles were mere small hurdles towards success.

I believe that the sense of inclusion, plus the feeling of confidence and empowerment fostered by my mentor, and also the encouragement from everyone in ITC, is reflective of the organization's strong culture of diversity and inclusion, and equal growth platform for all irrespective of function or gender.

I also keep writing my goals both short-term and long-term, both personal and professional, and keep updating the same once achieved. This reminds me of my aspirations and enables me to excel in whatever I do.

Food and Beverage Industry: A Gender Parity Initiative

Here is an example in the aligned food and beverage industry that is worth emulation. While it is more often than not the case that multinational companies tend to push ahead deadlines when it comes to issues like gender parity, the restaurant company YUM! Brands recently actually brought forward the gender party deadline from 2030 to 2025.

As per its Global Citizenship & Sustainability Report (2020),

> In 2020, we increased the number of women in senior leadership globally to 47%, accelerating our target to achieve gender parity in leadership globally by 2025. Our previous aspiration was in line with Paradigm for Parity's goal to advance women to senior roles and achieve gender parity in leadership globally by 2030.[1]

Perceiving gender parity as a strong business case, the YUM! Brands, Inc. in India has made notable strides in diversity and inclusion practices, for example, its subsidiary KFC has an all-female 15-member team in the city of Hyderabad. In addition, under the umbrella of the diversity and inclusion programme known as Kshamata, KFC aims for more than 5,000 women team members to be able to operate 70 KFCs by 2024, which means training them for restaurant leadership roles. By doing so, the number of women in the workforce at their restaurants is projected to double by 2024.

In order to encourage more women to join the company at leadership levels YUM! is in partnership with the Indian School of Management (ISH), Gurgaon (a higher education institute founded by Dilip Puri, who was a former Managing Director and Regional Vice President of Starwood Hotels and Resorts South Asia). Together YUM! and ISH have floated an 11-month management development programme for young female aspirants, which will train them to take up the position of KFC Area Coaches once they graduate, which means independently handling two to three KFC outlets. The training programme will sharpen their leadership skills by focussing on operations know-how and polishing their business and financial acumen.

Said Kunal Vasudeva, Chief Operating Officer at ISH,

> The postgraduate programme is designed to help accelerate the career of young professionals in the newer normal, and with KFC

---

[1]https://www.yum.com/wps/wcm/connect/yumbrands/9f83071e-35d7-4782-a6af-4f70eee 367e8/2020+Citizenship+Report_People-1.pdf?MOD=AJPERES&CVID=nHB3dEI, accessed on 8 November 2022, p. 16.

India as our partners, we are excited to be taking our programme's vision a step further – to invite more women candidates and prepare them for leadership roles in the industry.[2]

The female aspirants who apply to this programme have been jointly recruited by YUM! and ISH against certain parameters of merit and experience. After successful completion of the programme, 50% of the fee is to be reimbursed over two years of employment with KFC as an Area Coach. Said Anshu Poonia who is enrolled in this course:

> I was working as an assistant manager food and beverages in Hyderabad. A position of Area Coach would have taken another 7 years or so. This programme seemed too good to be true, so I did call up someone at KFC for further verification as there are so many scams these days. Anyway, there were several rounds of interviews, the last one being quite nerve-wracking as there were 15 male interviewers on the zoom call. But in the end I was able to convince them of my candidature.

In spite of this upskilling scheme – which seems too good to be true – leading to the enviable Area Coach post, fewer woman candidates applied than had been anticipated. Dilip Puri said:

> We are really excited about the course that we are implementing for the YUM! candidates to take them to the next level of leadership. We have an exciting syllabus for them, excellent faculty and there is a portion of hands-on training too. I do believe more candidates would have joined this training had the criterion for recruitment – set at four years work experience – was not so stringent. As you know in India there is quite a lot of family pressure to get married and have children for young women in the age range of 24 to 30. So a female candidate who would be about 26 years old, would most likely be married and thinking of expanding her family. At such a stage in her life to leave a full time job for an 11-months training leading to a post-graduate diploma is quite risky and may not excite her.

Anshu was one of the few candidates ready to take the plunge and take a risk. She said,

---

[2]https://indiaeducationdiary.in/kfc-india-extends-growth-opportunities-for-women-leaders-with-their-first-area-coaches-programme-for-women/, accessed on 8 November 2022.

I left a paid job to take up this training. One has to be willing to make sacrifices for a good position. Many women want a good salary but won't step out of the comfort zone. I believe that as you are moving up you are taking someone else's position. You have to make to own space. The only real challenge I see in this industry is that men often are not keen to report to a women. My father was in the army and there I saw that soldiers salute a women superior proudly. So I guess this industry has a glamorous side, but an ugly side too.

To sum up, while the intentions of a multinational company may be commendable, with a suitable rollout to encourage more women at the top, the country context of India with its patriarchal norms, in which the woman is expected to be the primary care giver at home for children and ageing in-laws, can prove to be challenging.

Chapter 5

Recommendations

Up to now in this study, many of the barriers and enablers to leadership growth have been highlighted. In this chapter, recommendations are put forward (a) by the study respondents themselves – to industry leaders, the firm, the industry, and also the Government of India, (b) suggestions by the author to policy makers and industry leaders, and (c) suggestions by the author to scholars in terms of future studies.

By Study Respondents

Leadership Level

Gender sensitization:

- 'My recommendation would be first, to respect and follow the law and second, to remove bias.' (R4-S-M)

Says Ranju Alex, Area Vice President – South Asia, Marriott International,

> We need to do away with gender bias. I seriously want to tell leaders that there are a lot of good women talent out there. Do not be judgemental and make your decision based on gender. Make you decision on the basis of the quality that the person brings to the table. I have had several encounters where people even without meeting a candidate say they do not want a female candidate. My only advice is: go by the individual, do not go by gender.

Dilip Puri says,

> One needs to sensitize men to accept shared parenting and an equal respect for the spouse's career. We had a very smart lady who was our director of sales and marketing, who had

Gender Equity in Hospitality: The Case of India, 49–60
Copyright © 2023 by Payal Kumar
Published under exclusive licence by Emerald Publishing Limited
doi:10.1108/978-1-80382-665-320231005

aspirations to be a general manager. And her husband was also a hotelier. However, her new job required her to move to another city. And I remember counseling them both, and they jointly agreed that she's got the better opportunity, so she's definitely shifting and that he will try and find an opportunity there. And because she was going to the general manager, she could take her daughter with her.

Enabling women to balance work and family:

- 'I think the first thing I would say is that they need to respect women, even her personal life, you have to look at it in totality, look at the other side of life also because that is the reason why she's not coming into the mainstream.' (R12-S-F)
- 'So your policy should be such that you are also keeping her personal life in mind, it has to encourage her and not leave her family and pretend to be a man.' (R12-S-F)
- 'If we're talking about a hotel the woman has to leave her family, the way policies are made she should also be allowed to take her entire family with her, live in the hotels, be given all the benefits, everything, and be provided the same salary too.' (R12-S-F)

Monisha Dewan speaks of women-centric leadership:

We have to allow for diversity. In other words, for women it is not that they should become like men, but rather that they should be allowed to make their choices. For example, we should say to first-time mothers, 'Hey, welcome back to work, how can we make it comfortable back home for you? What is the help you need there?'

Prevent sexual harassment:

- 'Consider the issue of prevention of sexual harassment at workplace.' (R15-S-M)
- 'We need real sensitization of the employees towards prevention of sexual harassment and its practice in daily life.' (R15-S-M)
- 'We need to fight against physical or sexual abuse. There are laws there but they need to be adhered to and really followed.' (R13-S-M)

Good HR policies:

- 'From a human resource stand point, gender and diversity-related policy and programmes clearly lay down the ground rules in terms of the numbers and ratios that must be satisfied for a balanced score-card.' (R2-S-M)

Says Aradhana Lal,

I think there a very simple answer to creating policies that support inclusion and diversity is a line borrowed from Nike i.e. JUST DO IT. So my advice with regard to inclusion and diversity, to the leaders in our sector or in any other sector is – JUST DO IT. Don't hesitate, keep an open mind and open the doors to your organization. You can do your homework and come up with the practical solutions to make sure that your company is culturally ready to welcome people. It's about building culture. And it's about having the courage to just do it. Very simple.

Firm Level

Assess and audit working conditions for women:

- 'We need to assess the situation and the conditions of work and see whether they are compliant with the biological, mental, and emotional needs of women or not.' (R22-S-F)
- 'Infrastructure needs to be reassessed by some sort of a certification body to ensure compliance with the expectations of a woman.' (R22-S-F)
- 'Do a market study for the compensation and also for the safety and security of the entire staff.' (R6-S-M)
- 'We must have in place gender neutral work environment at all levels.' (R1-S-F)
- 'It's things like having a sanitary and napkin dispenser in all public washrooms for any sort of emergency. How difficult is that for something like that to be institutionalized?' (R22-S-F)
- 'I think more than reducing the number of work hours, ensuring flexibility in work hours is a better approach.' (R2-S-M)
- 'More flexibility provided in terms of work hours and I'm talking about across the board because right now the industry is losing talent to other sectors because of our crazy work hours.' (R14-S-M)

Says Meena Bhatia,

> I would like to reiterate a suggestion made by a former Direc-tor General of Tourism demanding an audit of workplaces for gender-friendly practices and the workplace environment. If we critically analyze our workplace infrastructure, dressing and uniforms, aesthetics, processes, etc. we will find several hidden bias in things such as seating, uniforms, designs, etc. We must have in place gender neutral work environment at all levels.

Reservations for women?
Opinions are divided here with those who are proponents for reservations (similar to the mandated female representation on company boards as per the Companies Act, 2013), and others who are against this arguing that gender neutral policies and opportunities are more important.

- 'There should be a representation at the top of at least two, three heads of divi-sion as women, so that then they consciously look out for women.' (R9-M-F)

- 'Make the workplace conducive for lady workers and colleagues: maybe even provide some reservation for ladies.' (R7-M-F)

Says Anika Gupta,

> Making reservations or allocating percentages of women as a fixated blanket policy may not work. It has to be imbibed as a culture, an intent, a consideration, a dynamic approach. However, there could be some set ups, institutions which may warrant a formal reservation matrix, which can be introduced in a time-bound manner, while keeping the threshold of talent and skill-set required for the job or the education program as applicable. In fact, once it makes an impact to the overall health of the ecosystem, it may be removed, to restore balance of a new order. Organizations are increasingly realizing that having a gender-balanced work force gives a valuable perspective which could get missed out in a gender lopsided team. Moreover, customer landscape is also changing with decision making getting re-distributed across genders. Given this, it is in the interest of an organization to speak a language that appeals to all genders. Ultimately our actions should be motivated by equal opportunity, yet excellence-based systems.

Anuraag Bhatnagar adds,

> Just like board of directors in companies are expected to have at-least 30% women representation, something similar needs to be put in place at the industry level. Most progressive organizations are already ensuring gender diversity at all levels. However, we still need industry benchmark requiring every organization to have certain percentage of women in their leadership positions. Furthermore, we also need to institutionalize options such as work from home and flexible work-hours. In my own experience, at least 70% of people who are working from home are able to perform better. With technological innovations it is possible to bring in more focus, align priorities, ensuring non-duplication of efforts, conduct faster virtual meetings, etc.

Increase the Diversity Pool:

Kanika Hasrat says,

> I believe the way to increase the pool size and attract the best of the talents is to let it percolate it from the top. And when I say the

top I mean let it begin from the educational institutes. The hotel management institutes that we have from where we get most of the management trainees and other graduates – I mean why not begin from there? We will have to tap the talent just when they are starting. If we educate them really on what it means to be working in the industry and train them about what it really is to be a part of this space then I am very sure that we will see a lot of young women coming in and rising through the ranks. I believe what we lack is clear communication about what this industry is. If we keep loosing good talent from these campuses then I don't think the situation is going to be any different than what it is right now.

Industry Level

National-level benchmarking:

- 'We still need an industry benchmark requiring every organization to have certain percentage of women in their leadership positions.' (R2-S-M)
- 'We need to believe that individual organizations will have to have stated goals that can be measured to make sure that they can see more women at the leadership.' (R14-S-M)
- 'The industry can introduce a framework where leadership roles get defined in organizations at proper levels at corporate levels.' (R11-S-M)

International benchmarking:

- 'We need to learn from European countries like Sweden, Germany and Switzerland, which have started moving towards 6 hours a day work rule that gives individuals time for their personal life.' (R8-M-F)

Says Anika Gupta,

India is a vibrant diaspora for businesses today. We are in an amazing growth and learning curve. Yet, it may be worthwhile to learn from hospitality industries of leading global markets of Europe or the US, or other select countries of Asia in terms of woman leader representation in the hospitality industry. Are we worse off or are we better off? If we are doing better off than nothing like it, but if we are worse off than Europe or USA or a leading market of Asia, then it would be prudent for various stakeholders to take into cognizance findings of the study and consciously implement select recommendations as applicable.

Preventing human trafficking and child labour:

- 'We need to begin by acknowledging the problem of human trafficking and child labour in the unorganized sector of the industry and thereafter take steps to rectify it.' (R15-S-M)

Nikhil Sharma says,

> The problem of human trafficking within the industry becomes
> prominent in unorganized sectors within the hospitality industry.
> Hospitality is a labour-intensive industry. If you were to go to
> beyond the big hotel and survey smaller aggregator hotels you'll
> end up finding high instances of human trafficking and child
> labour. For example, a fourteen-year-old Ramu serving tea or ice
> to the customers may be a common sight, but is something we
> need to rectify. At the moment we are not doing enough to address
> the human trafficking problem in the industry. Just because the
> problem doesn't pertain to the organized sector, we should not shy
> away from taking a lead in addressing it.

Systemic reforms and women centricity:

- 'I would recommend them to walk the talk and avoid mere tokenisms for creating a more diverse and inclusive workforce, which can only happen when there is an initiative from the entire industry. Gender inequity is a deeply rooted, systemic issue, and therefore requires work at the foundational level.' (R18-S-F)

Says Nikhil Sharma,

> My own suggestion for the industry would be to pay more
> attention to two issues – (i) Sexual harassment at workplace
> and (ii) human trafficking and child labour in the unorganized sector. Consider prevention of sexual harassment at
> workplace. I would differentiate between a formal implementation versus actual following through by gender sensitization and incorporating daily life practices at the workplaces.
> We in industry need to constantly ask ourselves, are we being
> an evangelist? Do we have the posters out there? Are there
> enough PoSH trainings? Are we speaking about these issues?
> Do women know about their rights and grievance mechanisms? Is it part of the induction system? Is it part of their
> daily life? We need to go beyond merely putting a tick mark
> against government-mandated compliances. We need real sensitization of the employees towards prevention of sexual harassment and its practice in daily life.

Government Level

Support localization:

- 'HRD Ministry-led initiatives ought not just educate, but hire too (using gender-based affirmative action, based on minimum qualification and merit):

That will increase traction and improve the funnel for participation at the workplace by women.' (R7-M-F)

- 'Clearly, incentivising education for the girl child is very important, including giving them scholarships all the way to college – of course subject to certain terms and conditions, such as excellent academic performance.' (R10-S-M)

Says Bindu Jacob Mathew, a doctoral scholar, who was former Corporate Head – Sustainability at Mahindra Holidays & Resorts India,

> If a hotel is in a remote location the Government needs to get involved and support the locals in terms of enhancing their skills, because why would a hospitality company invest so much? Especially so in regions where the local language is not English. So in remote locations you have to have women-centric policies which support women both at the entry level, and mid-career too when maximum dropouts occur.

Recommendations for Policy Makers and Industry Leaders in India

Based largely on the first order themes that emerged from this study, as represented by the thematic tree (Fig. 2), here are the study recommendations for policy makers and industry leaders in India:

Entry Barriers

For policy makers:

1. Encourage employability for economically weak females and provide scholarships and fee concessions at leading hotel management institutes.
2. The government to allocate more of the corporate social responsibility (CSR) budget to apprenticeship programmes such as *Hunar se Rozgar.*

For industry leaders:

1. Provide sponsorships for economically weak females to study at hotel management institutes.
2. Provide such students with relevant mentorship too.

Quitting/Taking A Break After Childbirth

For policy makers:

1. Commission an in-depth study to understand the effect of post-natal job losses.

2. Commission a study to understand the effect of the hospitality industry on the 'missing female workforce' – of women who don't join the industry due to high entry barriers.
3. Local government to create communal crèches and provide state-wise support for women going back to work after childbirth.
4. State governments to also provide additional medical allowance for medical complications and at-risk pregnancies, and free counselling (for both women and their husbands/partners) for mental health-related issues owing to post-partum depression.
5. Create an advisory protocol for crèches in locations with more than 50 women in one office complex.
6. Enact legislation to provide for paternity leave in the private sector too. Currently, only central government employees are entitled to paternity leave of 15 days.

For industry leaders:

1. Return-to-work programmes to support and encourage return after maternity breaks.
2. Training for line managers and senior executives on how to overcome unconscious gendered biases.
3. Updated skill matrices to be worked out between line managers and the human resources department for maximizing efficacy in post-partum working situation (such as less or no travel for 3 months and flexible working hours through a hybrid model).
4. Aggressive upskilling opportunities for returning women, following a post-partum HR profiling of the employee, especially as studies indicate that taking a maternity break has a long-term negative impact on gender wage gap.
5. Organizations to draft progressive maternal and paternal leave policy for the mother and father (for couples who are colleagues), to shoulder equal home and work responsibilities.
6. Utilize a part of the CSR budget to provide crèche for kids at work, subject to threshold workforce size.
7. Exit interviews to be reviewed by top management to identify structural changes to address attrition after childbirth.

Lack of Mobility for Different Job Locations

For industry leaders:

1. Leverage the hybrid working trend to widen the geographical reach of recruits.
2. When the woman is being transferred provide an option for her husband (colleague) to move with her, in the same way, this courtesy should be

offered to male employees. Also, she can be provided extra incentives if her family does not shift with her, such as two trips to visit her family annually. Furthermore, industry leaders need to recognize that many women are the main or even sole bread earner for the family. (There was a 39% increase in the number of single women in India between the 2001 and 2011 census.)

Power of Networking

For policy makers:
Create an Ombudsperson on the Ministry of Tourism portal to address the grievances of women in the tourism and hospitality industry.

For industry leaders:

1. Take initiatives for women to share their experiences across multiple locations within an organization.
2. Arrange for mentors and sponsors for high potential candidates.
3. Industry bodies such as FHRAI, WICCI, FAITH, AIMA to organize speed networking events with woman leaders. Greater gendered representation is required in these bodies too.
4. For women to understand the importance of networking, arrange for panel discussions with the above industry bodies.

Work–Life Pressure Challenges

For policy makers:

Evaluate the option of 4.5-day work week policy, starting with women first.

For industry leaders:

1. Policies relating to flexible work arrangements to focus on productivity, rather than time or location.
2. Flexibility in working hours through a hybrid workspace (physical office and virtual space).
3. Systemic support for women balancing work and home, such as the option of a 4.5-day work-week for young mothers or for those tending to terminally ill family members.
4. Organizational recognition and praise of employee extra-role behaviour goes a long way (Chang & Uen, 2022). So for those female employees working long hours and that too not being able to enjoy festival season with the family due to peak client servicing time, their work could be recognized and appreciated.

Gender Stereotypes by Colleagues

For policy makers:

1. Diversity and inclusion training curriculum to be mandatorily included for students at all hotel management institutes.
2. A government body should compile and share an annual report on diversity and inclusion indicators in the industry (e.g. of gender pay parity and gender representation at all levels), with an analysis of how well companies are performing. This could be based on the environmental, social, and governance (ESG) report compiled by hotels, and on other measures too.

For industry leaders:

1. Diversity and inclusion trainings to be regularly provided to all staff to avoid gender stereotyping.
2. Create a framework for capturing and addressing instances of gender stereotype/discrimination.
3. Appoint top leadership as chief mentor/chairperson of 'Women Welfare at Work' forums.
4. Have targeted women representation across all levels of leadership.
5. Share and disclose best practices of gender-friendly policies in a transparent manner in the annual ESG report, which is freely available to all.

Gender Stereotypes by Organizations

For policy makers:

Enforce 40% reservation women in all tourism and hospitality organizations, and provide organizations with a tax deduction incentive for achieving this target.

For industry leaders:

1. Build up gender diversity strategy after capturing data on the number of female employees function-wise, details of pay parity, the number of women in the executive committee, etc.
2. Align diversity goals with strategy, including strategy planning initiatives that bring in women to more 'hard core' functions such as finance, strategy, and business development, rather than the only more 'traditional functions' such as human resources.

Fewer Role Models for Women

For policy makers:

1. Mandate 25% of ministerial positions in the Ministry of Tourism for women by 2025.

2. Provide stamp duty relief for woman hotel owners. In case of company ownership, have a minimum 51% shareholding by women to qualify for property tax concessions.
3. Hotel owning company having more than mandated number of women directors on board to qualify for corporate tax rebate.

For industry leaders:

1. Company commitment to be defined at board level and executive level.
2. Develop a woman focussed mid-management talent pool for transition into leadership roles based on merit, in order to manage the 'leaky pipeline problem'.
3. Assess annually the number of women in leadership positions and board representation, and capture the same in annual ESG reports.
4. Create a woman-only shadow board to develop a new/different perspective.
5. Promote visibility of role models through suitable external PR and internal communication tools.

Pay Parity

For policy makers:

1. Envision a 100% pay parity by 2025, with severe penalties on entities indulging in pay disparity for the same work.
2. Third party company to assess salaries and pay disparity and provide a periodic report to the government.

For industry leaders:

1. Capture pay parity on an annual basis in ESG reports, drawing on pay parity audits.
2. Periodic evaluation of recruitment and promotion policies by a third party consultancy company (in order to eliminate bias in the report).

Recommendations to Scholars for Further Research

Research on diversity in tourism and hospitality is gaining more traction. In a systematic review of the literature over two decades, it appears that while the research largely emanates from the United States, the United Kingdom, and China (Mohammadi, Bhati, & Ng, 2022), more recent scholarship is emerging from China, Taiwan, and Hong Kong, suggesting that equity concerns are becoming increasingly prominent across continents (Manoharan & Singal, 2017). This study adds to the literature of the Global South, and in doing so showcases the importance of the national and cultural contextualization of a phenomenon.

Further research could be conducted on:

(a) The role of peer mentoring – colleagues can often help to navigate complexities of the workplace.
(b) The role of informal mentoring – in cases where the formal mentor is not providing guidance to the fullest of expectations, an informal mentor selected by the mentee could enable the mentoring and learning to continue, thus possibly reducing any feelings of professional frustration.
(c) The role of social support from both the supervisor and colleagues in the workplace – studies suggest that positive interpersonal relationships at work can reduce the effect of work–life conflict on occupational stress (Richard, 2021).
(d) Intersectionalities – more research is required on topics such as 'women and caste' or 'women with disabilities', or even on women who face societal stigma due to divorce, remarriage, or because they may opt not to marry.
(e) The state of employment of transgender people in the tourism and hospitality industry – while the Transgender Persons (Protection of Rights) Bill, 2019, prohibits discrimination in terms of employment, what in fact is the real picture?
(f) Collecting pan-India data on the actual number of women in the workforce at different levels of seniority (see Appendix Table A2).

Chapter 6

Discussion and Conclusion

People-centric Industry Vying for Talent

Hospitality is an industry that is hugely people-dependent, and it goes to stand that attracting talent in the market is fundamental for success. Says Benoît-Etienne Domenget,

> Having spent the last 20 years in that industry, I had the opportunity to experience how much people make a difference. People in our industry are more than a key success factor, they are the very heart of our DNA.[1]

In this people-centric industry that is growing in leaps and bounds post-COVID-19 pandemic, industry leaders cannot afford to be complacent, but rather need to keep reinventing to move with the times. Says Anuraag Bhatnagar,

> It is estimated that by 2028 the tourism industry will contribute $460 billion towards India's GDP, and that by 2029 it is estimated that this will account for 53 million jobs. He adds that the industry needs to sensitize itself to new comers, and display more patience while inducting and training them in their new roles, while creating new pathways for their learning and growth.[2]

This growth seems to be exponential. Says Mandeep Lamba, President – (South Asia) HVS Anarock,

---

[1] file:///C:/Users/ish080/Downloads/The%20State%20of%20Hospitality%202022%20-%20LD%20(3).pdf, accessed on 5 January 2023, p. 16.
[2] file:///C:/Users/ish080/Downloads/The%20State%20of%20Hospitality%202022%20-%20LD%20(3).pdf, accessed on 5 January 2023, p. 14.

Gender Equity in Hospitality: The Case of India, 61–68
Copyright © 2023 by Payal Kumar
Published under exclusive licence by Emerald Publishing Limited
doi:10.1108/978-1-80382-665-320231006

India, one of the fastest growing economies in the world, is expected to become the third largest by 2030. With its resilience to global headwinds thus far and a prominent role in the G20, the country will play an important part in shaping the global economy going forward. This is good news for the country's tourism industry, as both inbound and outbound travel are expected to increase significantly in the coming years. To be part of this growth story, all major international hotel chains are increasing their presence in the country.[3]

Not only is the industry growing rapidly, but it is transforming in multiple ways. For example, there has been a spurt in domestic tourism, leisure destination, part-business–part-leisure travel (bleisure), eco-friendly and rural tourism, sustainable tourism, and also medical tourism.

In this context of an ever-expanding industry that is seeing tectonic shifts, it is hoped that this study has provided a deeper understanding of the existing scenario by penetrating the surface of everyday practices and discourses, to reveal deeply embedded practices, viewpoints, and biases. After all gender, as a socially constructed phenomenon, permeates all levels of society, so much so that in an ongoing study on the banking sector in India by Payal Mukherjee, doctoral scholar, TISS, Mumbai, gender as a social construct was found to play an important role in the perpetuation of the glass ceiling phenomenon.

Themes in Relation to the Life Cycle of a Woman

In this study, barriers for entering the workforce and also for climbing the hierarchical level were found at three levels of analysis: (a) individual level, (b) group level, and (c) firm level (see Fig. 3). Many of the barriers to woman leadership are common across the globe, such as the double bind:

> You will need to have those skills to be assertive at the same time be feminine. If you have an opinion as a woman and you're very forceful then men feel a bit threatened. (R9-M-F)

Others barriers were more unique to a patriarchal and masculine society.

Drawing from the themes in the thematic tree, here is an analysis of the findings in the framework of the life cycle of a female employee.

---

[3]https://www.outlookindia.com/outlook-spotlight/-in-conversation-with-mr-mandeep-lamba-as-he-about-the-impact-of-global-hospitality-on-the-indian-market-news-246315, accessed on 5 January 2023.

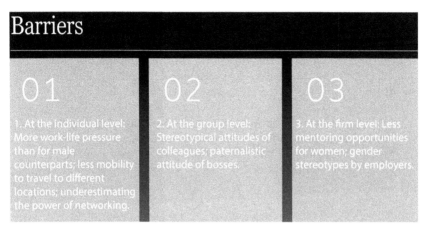

Fig. 3.   Indicative Barriers at Three Levels of Analyses. *Source*: Author's own.

Entry Level Barriers

The social system in India is still typically patriarchal and inequitable for women. In fact, often parents, in-laws, and even extended family members have a say in major life decisions of young women, such as marriage and career aspirations (Jejeebhoy, Santhya, Acharya, & Prakash, 2013). So entrenched are gender and familial roles in India that those who violate them often attract the disapproval and in extreme situations, even the wrath of family members. The stigma of the hospitality industry not being a suitable career track for women is rife, especially in South India, thus preventing women from joining. In the state of Kerala, girls are not even allowed to work in bars as doing so is a violation of the Foreign Liquor Rules, 1953.

Attrition After Childbirth

A recent International Labour Organization report indicates that from 2005 to 2019 the percentage of Indian women participating in the labour force dropped by a staggering 10%.[4] This is the largest dropout of any country in the world during the same time period. One reason for this trend is the twin pressures of work and home, where the working woman is simultaneously expected to be a model employee at work and also the primary caregiver at home. In fact, the most cited reason for a career break for Indian women is the predominance of family responsibilities including childcare, eldercare, and also spousal relocation (Ravindran & Baral, 2014).[5]

---

[4]http://data.worldbank.org/indicator/SL.TLF.CACT.FE.ZS
[5]See Appendix Table A2 on employee data on gender representation, 2022, which includes data on attrition.

Reflecting earlier studies, this study too shows that managing the twin challenges of both work and family is a major reason why many women drop out of
work after childbirth. In order to maintain a balance, good support from families
becomes critically important (Bhattacharya, Mohapatra, & Bhattacharya, 2018),
as does good support from the employer (Kumar, Chakraborty, & Kumar, 2020).
One respondent who has been in the industry for about 15 years says,

> In my experience, women who are at senior leadership position
> have had to make a lot of family and health sacrifices to reach
> there. For example, they may be divorced or may have never
> thought of getting married to concentrate more on their profes-
> sional life.

Employers may do well to think out of the box and leverage work-from-home
practices (for some functions) to support women in career successes in this male-
dominated industry (Burleson, Major, & Eggler, 2021). Also, they would need
to add more support systems at the workplace, for example, crèche facilities. A
recent study suggests that perceptions of pregnancy discrimination by women are
moderated by perceived supervisor support. Thus, competitive maternity benefits
would need to be paired with supportive supervisors for working mothers to be
retained in the workplace (Paustian-Underdahl, 2022).

Employers may also consider sensitizing fathers to avail of paternity leave,
and other leave that is required for the family, rather than placing the onus on
their spouse. Research suggests that longer leaves for fathers, say in the form of
paternity leave, leads to mothers taking less leave from work (Pylkkänen & Smith,
2002).

Barriers for Mid-level Managers

Invisible barriers of organizational bias include stereotypical perceptions of an
ideal leader as being goal-oriented, ambitious, and assertive (more male-like
attributes).[6] Due to this bias, it is possible that fewer women are singled out for
the leadership track. As per Eagly and Karau's (2002) Role Congruity Theory,
rethinking the leadership qualities required in an industry could reduce bias
against woman leaders.

Furthermore, this study reflects others that suggest that women receive inconsistent mentoring support compared to their male counterparts, in the form of
both career and psycho-social support. And yet adequate mentoring can help
women navigate the challenges of work–life interface (Blake-Beard et al., 2017).
Mentoring is a critical process to build confidence and positive identities in
women by industry mentors (Murrell & Onosu, 2022). Kumar and Blake-Beard
(2012) assert that women need to recognize the power of building up a network

---

[6]See Appendix Table A3 for respondents' views on the ideal leader.

of mentors, as within a 'feminine model of mentoring, human growth occurs through relational connections with others' (p. 30).

- 'If there's a young woman who comes in and she's looking at this, she's wondering, how do I get that presence? How do I develop that gravitas? How do I get the world to see me? She needs help. She needs mentorship.' (R12-S-F)
- 'Mentorship also becomes crucial when a professional is learning and preparing to go up the ladder – in that case it becomes very important.' (R23-M-M)
- 'It is important to get feedback and mentorship from one's peers and former colleagues.' (R2-S-M)

This situation is further aggravated by less number of female role models in the upper echelons. Drawing on leader–membership exchange theory, a recent hospitality study strongly suggests that subordinates do learn by observing and mimicking role models, more so if they are in the in-group of the supervisor (Xiao & Mao, 2022). In other words, role models play an important role in the social learning process. Some women may have low self-esteem and thus be subjected to imposter syndrome, whereby they reach a senior level and they think maybe they didn't deserve it (says Ritu Verma).

It seems likely that a few women may underestimate the power of networking. Says Zubin Mehta, Managing Director at Radisson Hotel Group,

> Expanding your contacts can open doors to new opportunities for business, career advancement, personal growth, or simply new knowledge. Active networking helps to keep you top of mind when opportunities such as job openings arise and increases your likelihood of receiving introductions to potentially relevant people or even a referral. Don't forget that many jobs don't even get advertised – particularly as your career advances – so being a recognized part of networks is a keyway to gain access to opportunities that you might not have otherwise.

In the meantime, in an industry where transfers to different locations often enhances the possibility of moving into leadership positions, the ease of mobility of male colleagues appears to be an undue advantage. Says Bindu Jacob Mathew,

> If you want to grow in the organization, one would have to get yourself a management degree. The other is you wish you have to be willing to travel. Like you cannot just stay in one location and expect to like climb the ladder. It is imperative that for you to grow, let's say I'm located in Chennai and I'm handling a certain portfolio. Now they say yeah sure your work is fantastic and we would love to promote you, but you do not have any vacancy in Chennai. Would you be willing to move to another location, say Bangalore?

Conclusion

Many of the barriers mentioned in this study are also common to women in other industries in India (refer to the roundtable discussion). However, there are certain professions in which women have managed to break the glass ceiling, for example, India has the highest number of female pilots in the world at 12.4% which is twice the global average, even though this is a profession that involves 100% travelling and also shift work. Financial services and the banking sector is another area where women have stormed the male bastion and are heading banks and financial services. The most recent example is of the appointment of Vishaka Mulye as the first woman CEO of Aditya Birla Capital. In both these examples, women have managed to soar to leadership positions in spite of the gender stereotypes that 'women can't read maps' and that 'women are not good at maths and number crunching'. So why is it that women in the tourism and hospitality industry can't fly as high?

This study suggests that what perhaps stands out for the hospitality industry in India is the entry-level barrier due to the stereotype that this is not a suitable industry for women. This study notes that long working hours, and also the social taboo of women working in bars, etc. are distinct entry barriers. One can only conjecture about the 'missing women' – in other words, those that want to join the industry, but who are discouraged from doing so by their family. There is no way to quantify the number of these potential hires. It is worthy to point out that post-liberalization in other industries such as information technology, women have been entering in large droves.

This study also notes that at the mid-management level many women drop out because juggling the pressures of both family and work becomes too much, thus creating a 'leaky pipeline problem' – where there are not enough female candidates to recommend for more senior positions.

> In traditional Indian culture, most marriages are arranged, i.e. they are negotiated by parents and extended family who screen potential spouses. In these cases, marriage is seen as a union between two families, not just two individuals. Within marriage, there are a number of expectations of Indian women. They are expected to place their families first; careers should be secondary; they are responsible for care of the children and aging parents. So Indian women face the same work-family balancing act that women around the world face, compounded by culture. (Blake-Beard et al., 2017, p. 35)

Another unique finding is that in this industry upward growth becomes next to impossible unless candidates are up for relocation. This was brought out clearly in Chapter 4 in the case of Amandeep Kaur who worked her way up from a housekeeping management trainee to General Manager after several geographical relocations.

In this study, there were some respondents who were of the opinion that there was a need to be gender agnostic or gender neutral and not offer any concession to female candidates or employees. In an ideal world where the playing field is level, this makes sense. But we do not live in an ideal world. For example, there was a *gendered impact on employment during the COVID-19 pandemic, with proportionately more women than men losing their jobs in India, and also their chances of being re-employed being comparatively less* (Deshpande, 2020). Thus, what is required for women to break the glass ceiling is not only talent, drive, and self-belief, but also deep structures of organizational and familial support.

In other words, there are deep-rooted issues that need to be tackled such as unconscious bias, and the need to ensure that each employee feels safe and appreciated in the work environment regardless of gender identity. Naturally, biases cannot be eradicated quickly, but rather require deep understanding and reform. Till then, effective measures need to be taken which promote women as leaders in the organizations.

So what if nothing is done to eradicate these biases? 'Hospitality is a feminized industry, in terms of the participation of women, but highly masculine in that men and male values predominate in management positions' (Segovia-Pérez, Figueroa-Domecq, Fuentes-Moraleda, & Muñoz-Mazón, 2019, p. 6). If organizations continue to reward traditional masculine leadership by encouraging individual successes and hyper-competition over more collaborative achievements, this tends to fuel ideals of masculinity, creating environments where women may feel threatened or isolated.[7] What is required is building a more equitable workplace culture where all employees feel comfortable.

So how does one overcome the bias of 'think manager, think male?' Industry leaders would need to reflect on whether a leader necessarily has to be an agentic male, simply because this has been the precedent in the industry so far? They may want to move from this auto-pilot mode, introspect, and rethink the leadership qualities required in the industry, using a different lens, for example, contemplating a style of leadership that may be more androgynous in nature (an amalgamation of sex-role identities and styles). Androgynous styles of leadership have been documented to lead to better decision-making, more creativity and innovation, and increased team cooperation (Blake-Beard, Shapiro, & Ingols, 2020).

Of course, the onus for ensuring gender parity is not only on industry leaders, policy makers, and the government. Women too can take charge to some extent by constant upskilling, building up a network constellation of formal, informal, and also peer mentors, being prepared to travel to different locations, and learning how to navigate office politics, for example, by understanding the complexities of impression management (Sanaria, 2016). Says Ranju Alex,

> My only advice has always been that – you have a spark which very few people has. You will work with bosses and colleague which might not support the spark but at the end of the day it's your spark, don't let it out.

---

[7]https://hbr.org/2023/01/research-what-fragile-masculinity-looks-like-at-work, accessed on 7 January 2023.

Says Monisha Dewan, 'Many young women are aspiring to grow into leadership roles. Their constant concern is their development, whether it is gaining knowledge or developing a strong executive presence. As a professional woman, it is important to raise your hand to be mentored and coached. Seeking feedback and guidance helps you gain perspective. To grow as a leader you need to be visible and you should be able to influence people around you. Networking is also a very important aspect which helps in influencing stakeholders and to understand their expectations. We have seen that men have an advantage when it comes to networking. They find it easier to network through informal meetings whereas women prioritize after work hours with family. Organizations should have a strong focus on creating mentoring, networking and coaching opportunities for women. My advice to young women who are entering leadership positions would be to remain authentic, to use their EQ to their benefit and have a clear vision of what they want to achieve. Manage your relationships well and build gravitas. Ask for the next role. Do not doubt yourself and remember, perfection can be achieved along the way. To be inspirational, continue learning, influence others, and definitely ensure that you grow more women leaders. Once you have gone into a leadership role, this is your responsibility!'

Overall, it is hoped that the themes from this study may serve to provide a profound understanding of the factors at play, leading to solutions that will lead to a more level playing field for women, so that one day 'women can wear their feminism, their confidence, their equality with pride' (Dilip Puri), and stand shoulder-to-shoulder with male colleagues to help build the industry into a formidable force. Not only is this the right thing to do from a justice lens, but the business case for gender equity speaks for itself. Says Jane Pendlebury, Chief Executive, Hospitality Professionals Association, UK,

> There is enough anecdotal data to suggest that businesses that prioritize inclusion and diversity are more successful than those that do not. In recent years, we've seen positive results from employing differently abled resources, which, when combined with diversity in race, gender, education, and skills, may help us reach new levels of efficiency.[8]

---

[8]file:///C:/Users/ish080/Downloads/The%20State%20of%20Hospitality%202022%20-%20LD%20(3).pdf, accessed on 5 January 2023, p. 20.

Appendix

Table A1. Student Perception of Internship Experience in the Hospitality Industry.

Survey Questions (Likert Scale)	(1) Strongly Disagree	(2) Disagree	(3) Neither Agree Nor Disagree	(4) Agree	(5) Strongly Agree
The working hours were too long	9	5	28	37	34
The working conditions were satisfactory	4	14	44	31	20
The colleagues were encouraging and good to work with	3	12	23	39	36
My direct supervisor was encouraging and good to work with	0	10	23	31	49
I felt I was doing work of value	6	11	25	36	35
I felt I was learning quite a lot on the job	1	11	28	30	43
I was challenged in a meaningful way on the job.	3	11	16	46	37
I was treated with respect by colleagues	4	11	29	38	31
I was treated with respect by clients	0	2	13	33	65
Was the industry exactly what you expected it to be?	7	18	37	28	23

Source: Author's own.

Table A2.   Employee Data on Gender Representation (2022).

	Lemon Tree Hotels Limited	Accor (AAPC India Hotel Management Pvt Ltd)	Radisson Hotel Group	Wyndham Hotels and Resorts (India/ Sri Lanka)	Leela Hotels
Entry level jobs – male	2,920	2,368	9,536	65%	1,796
Entry level jobs – female	386	414	1,362	35%	449
Mid-level jobs – male	1,749	1,435		55%	663
Mid-level jobs – female	152	248		30%	160
Senior level jobs – male	49	624	657	90%	90
Senior level jobs – female	7	140	61	10%	18
Percentage of women rejoining after maternity leave	90–95%	80%	98%	100%	75%
Attrition – male employees	28%	36%		15%	
Attrition – female employees	38%	46%			
CSR budget spent on women focussed initiatives	30–40%	32%	50%	–	

Source: Author's own.

Note: This survey was sent to several hotels. The ones represented in this table were kind enough to respond.

Table A3.   Respondents' Views on the Qualities of the Ideal Leader.

Responsible and caring	• 'Leadership personalities happily take up more responsibility.' (R2-S-M) • 'We evaluate talent on the belief that individuals who care for others, produce better results than those who are simply focused on the job at hand – to the exclusion of those they work or interact with.' (R19-S-M) • 'So leadership when you feel for the people, you have alignment with the organization and you have all the qualities that make a good leader, there's so many qualities.' (R21-S-M) • 'And somehow leaders should always be people who are very secure about themselves, who always have a plan, are inspirational and think about others rather than themselves.' (R12-S-F)
Rises to the occasion	• 'To me leaders are persons who can rise to the occasion.' (R2-S-M) • 'I think leadership is something if people have good communication skills, they have the ability to be able to handle the client on their own, it comes out over a period of time.' (R14-S-M) • 'A leader for me is a professional who is rising up to the occasion on the work site and delivering whenever he/she is required.' (R18-S-F)
Integrity	• 'We have to make sure that the integrity and the intensity in that person remains the same so that he/she goes far enough in their careers and not get settled for less.' (R4-S-M) • 'You have to think logically, you have to behave. You have to be aligned with the organization.' (R21-S-M) • 'I would look at confidence, I would look at belief in their own value system, integrity.' (R12-S-F)
Learning oriented	• 'So I would identify anybody who is willing to learn and re-learn and then adapt to our organisations environment and be ready to take up the efficiency to the next level.' (R18-S-F) • 'Never fail your organization.' (R7-M-F) • 'There is nobody who says, oh, I've learned everything. I know everything' (R17-S-F) • 'So I would identify anybody who is willing to learn and re-learn and then adapt to our organisations environment and be ready to take up the efficiency to the next level.' (R18-S-F) • 'That desire and that openness to say I will keep learning is a very important quality in a leader.' (R17-S-F)

Table A3.   (*Continued*)

Clear vision	• 'They have a clear line of sight and vision.' (R2-S-M) • 'So for us we do encourage people to take decisions on their own and I think that there are some ladies who are very comfortable in making those decisions.' (R14-S-M) • 'Aspiration must come from within, we identify potential on that basis.' (R7-M-F)
Highly enthusiastic	• 'So you know, I trust the person took that initiative and showed me the confidence.' (R6-S-M) • 'You have to be very cheerful, very energetic have very positive vibe and put the customer's need first.' (R9-M-F) • 'Recruitment process is not about one's personal background as much as how passionate one is in delivering according to organizational vision.' (R8-M-F)
Competent	• 'It is more critical that a leader displays competence.' (R2-S-M) • 'Whether they have business skills, whether they have people skills, relationship skills, communication skills, the right leadership consists of many things.' (R11-S-M) • 'It's the leadership qualities and the competencies that you have.' (R20-S-F) • 'By nature, there are some people with those skills and qualities with or without training; there are people that are very good with people.' (R9-M-F) • 'So I think for us it's all on merit and if I hire good people and they deserve to be in positions of leadership, it happens.' (R14-S-M) • 'We look at aspects such as – competencies, capabilities, past performances, 360 degree feedback, future potential.' (R2-S-M) • 'They have to have a good education background, they have to have the right exposure.' (R21-S-M)
Pushes oneself	• 'Willingness to quickly learn more and constantly challenges one's own self to push up the bar of excellence.' (R2-S-M) • 'We see if a person can take responsibility and deliver on it.' (R4-S-M) • 'Leadership personalities happily take up more responsibility.' (R2-S-M) • 'The leader should surely have the ability to learn and grow, the drive should be there.' (R4-S-M)

Innovative	• 'A leader should be constantly learning, innovating and evolving with time.' (R2-S-M)
	• 'There is a set of core competencies we look at, their adaptability to our values and culture, and then for senior leadership to a certain extent to draw on their past experiences for innovation.' (R13-S-M)
Identifies new leaders	• 'A job of a leader is to inspire others.' (R2-S-M)
	• 'We also look at leader as a person who takes responsibility for developing other leaders. The job of a leader is to identify and build more leaders.' (R2-S-M)
	• 'They always have a plan, are inspirational and think about others rather than themselves.' (R12-S-F)
	• 'Believes in "developing people around me."' (R7-M-F)
Hard working	• 'We pay at attention to how someone is driven and the level of passion and intensity demonstrated in work.' (R2-S-M)
	• 'For a woman especially she needs to be very dedicated and persevering because as you climb the ladder, you will find that there are more and more male colleagues and less and less women colleagues.' (R9-M-F)
Committed	• 'So they have to follow and to become a leader, you have to have sacrifices. You have to put people first.' (R21-S-M)
	• 'You need to be very committed, meaning there'll be a lot of pressure on you because you handle people, you handle customers.' (R9-M-F)
	• 'Displaying commitment to the team makes a difference.' (R7-M-F)
	• 'Display personal commitment to work, even while giving importance to family needs.' (R7-M-F)
Fighting spirit	• 'Are they able to speak with honesty, I definitely look for fire in the belly, are they passionate to grow?' (R12-S-F)
	• 'You will need to have those skills to be assertive at the same time as being feminine. If you have an opinion as a woman and you're very forceful then men feel a bit threatened.' (R9-M-F)
	• 'A leader as I see should be someone who should rise when we require him/her the most.' (R4-S-M)

(*Continued*)

Table A3.   (*Continued*)

Growth potential	• 'We have our annual reviews and we have a talent review done where we identify someone who is fast track and someone who has the spark to grow.' (R3-S-M)
Creative	• 'There are lots of opportunities and freedom to take up work and showcase one's work creativity.' (R8-M-F)
	• 'We would look at your calibre and creativity to give you an opportunity.' (R8-M-F)
Entrepreneurial and intrapreneurial	• 'So we are very entrepreneurial, it's really what you bring to the organization in terms of your role.' (R20-S-F)
	• 'The most important thing is that they keep an open mind and you get to see people's open mind by how much they participate in all activities at work.' (R12-S-F)

Source: Author's own.

Further Reading: Related Books by This Author

Kumar, P. (Ed.). (2015). *Unveiling women's leadership: Identity and meaning of leadership in India*. London: Springer International Publishing.

Kumar, P. (2016). *Indian women as entrepreneurs*. London: Springer International Publishing.

Kumar, P. (Ed.). (2018). *Exploring dynamic mentoring models in India*. London: Springer International Publishing.

Kumar, P., & Budhwar, P. (Eds.). (2020). *Mentorship-driven talent management: The Asian experience*. Bingley: Emerald Group Publishing.

Kumar, P., & Singh, G. (2020). *Gender equity in the boardroom: The case of India*. Bingley: Emerald Group Publishing.

References

Babcock, L., Gelfand, M., Small, D., & Stayn, H. (2006). Gender differences in the propensity to initiate negotiations. In D. D. Crèmer, M. Zeelenberg, & J. K. Murnighan (Eds.), *Social Psychology and Economics* (pp. 239–259). Mahwah, NJ: Lawrence Erlbaum.

Babcock, L., & Laschever, S. (2003). *Women don't ask.* Princeton, NJ: Princeton University Press.

Babcock, L., & Laschever, S. (2008). *Ask for it: How women can use the power of negotiation to get what they really want.* New York, NY: Bantam.

Bakker, I. (2007). Social reproduction and the constitution of a gendered political economy. *New Political Economy*, *12*(4), 541–556. http://doi.org/10.1080/13563460701661561

Baum, T. (2007). Human resources in tourism: Still waiting for change. *Tourism Management*, *28*(6), 1383–1399.

Bear, J. B., Cushenbery, L., London, M., & Sherman, G. D. (2017). Performance feedback, power retention, and the gender gap in leadership. *Leadership Quarterly*, *28*(6), 721–740. https://doi.org/10.1016/j.leaqua.2017.02.003

Bergmann, B. R. (1974). Occupational segregation, wages and profits when employers discriminate by race or sex. *Eastern Economic Journal*, *1*(2), 103–110.

Bertrand, M., & Hallock, K. F. (2001). The gender gap in top corporate jobs. *ILR Review*, *55*(1), 3–21. https://doi.org/10.1177/001979390105500101

Bhattacharya, S., Mohapatra, S., & Bhattacharya, S. (2018). Women advancing to leadership positions: A qualitative study of women leaders in IT and ITES sector in India. *South Asian Journal of Human Resources Management*, *5*(2), 150–172. https://doi.org/10.1177/2322093718782756

Blair-Loy, M. (2003). *Competing devotions: Career and family among women executives.* Cambridge, MA: Harvard University Press.

Blake-Beard, S., Halem, J., Archibold, E. E., Boncoeur, D. O., Burton, A. R., & Kumar, P. (2017). Mentoring relationships of professional Indian women: Extending the borders of our understanding at the intersection of gender and culture. In A. J. Murrell & S. Blake-Beard (Eds.), *Mentoring diverse leaders* (pp. 25–43). Oxfordshire: Routledge.

Blake-Beard, S., Shapiro, M., & Ingols, C. (2020). Feminine? Masculine? Androgynous leadership as a necessity in COVID-19. *Gender in Management: An International Journal*, *35*(7–8), 607–617.

Blayney, C., & Blotnicky, K. (2010). The impact of gender on career paths and management capability in the hotel industry in Canada. *Journal of Human Resources in Hospitality and Tourism*, *9*, 233–235.

Bligh, M., & Ito, A. (2017). Organizational processes and systems that affect women in leadership. In S. R. Madsen (Ed.), *Handbook of research on gender and leadership* (pp. 287–303). Cheltenham: Edward Elgar Publishing Limited.

Boone, J., Veller, T., Nikolaeva, K., Keith, M., Kefgen, K., & Houran, J. (2013). Rethinking a glass ceiling in the hospitality industry. *Cornell Hospitality Quarterly*, *54*(3), 230–239. http://doi.org/10.1177/1938965513492624

Bowles, H. R., Babcock, L., & Lai, L. (2007). Social incentives for gender differences in the propensity to initiate negotiations: Sometimes it does hurt to ask. *Organizational*

Behavior and Human Decision Processes, 103(1), 84–103. http://doi.org/10.1016/j. obhdp.2006.09.001

Bowles, H. R., Babcock, L., & McGinn, K. L. (2005). Constraints and triggers: Situational mechanics of gender in negotiation. *Journal of Personality and Social Psychology, 89*(6), 951–965.

Brownell, J. (1994). Women in hospitality management: General managers' perceptions of factors related to career development. *International Journal of Hospitality Management, 13*(2), 101–117. http://doi.org/10.1016/0278-4319(94)90032-9

Burleson, S. D., Major, D. A., & Eggler, K. D. (2021). Leveraging the new work from home normal to promote women's success in male-dominated fields. In P. Kumar, A. Agrawal, & P. Budhwar (Eds.), *Work from home: Multi-level perspectives on the new normal* (pp. 113–130). Bingley: Emerald Publishing. https://doi.org/10.1108/978-1-80071-661-220210007

Campos-Soria, J. A., García-Pozo, A., & Sánchez-Ollero, J. L. (2015). Gender wage inequality and labour mobility in the hospitality sector. *International Journal of Hospitality Management, 49*, 73–82. http://doi.org/10.1016/j.ijhm.2015.05.009

Campos-Soria, J. A., Marchante-Mera, A., & Ropero-García, M. A. (2011). Patterns of occupational segregation by gender in the hospitality industry. *International Journal of Hospitality Management, 30*(1), 91–102. http://doi.org/10.1016/j.ijhm.2010.07.001

Campos-Soria, J. A., Ortega-Aguaza, B., & Ropero-García, M. A. (2009). Gender segregation and wage difference in the hospitality industry. *Tourism Economics, 15*(4), 847–866. http://doi.org/10.5367/000000009789955152

Carvalho, I., Costa, C., Lykke, N., & Torres, A. (2019). Beyond the glass ceiling: Gendering tourism management. *Annals of Tourism Research, 75*, 79–91. http://doi.org/10.1016/j.annals.2018.12.022

Carvalho, I., Costa, C., Lykke, N., Torres, A., & Wahl, A. (2018). Women at the top of tourism organizations: Views from the glass roof. *Journal of Human Resources in Hospitality & Tourism, 17*(4), 397–422. http://doi.org/10.1080/15332845.2018.1449551

Catalyst. (2007). The bottom line: Corporate performance and women's representation on boards. Retrieved from https://www.catalyst.org/research/the-bottom-line-corporate-performance-and-womens-representation-on-boards/. Accessed on August 25, 2021.

Chang, H. C., & Uen, J. F. (2022). Shaping organizational citizenship behavior of new employees: Effects of mentoring functions and supervisor need for achievement. *SAGE Open, 12*(1), 1–11. https://doi.org/10.1177/21582440211068515

Chaudhary, M., & Gupta, M. (2010). Gender equality in Indian hotel industry – A study of perception of male and female employees. *International Journal of Hospitality and Tourism Systems, 3*, 31–41.

Cleveland, J. N., Vescio, T. K., & Barnes-Farnell, J. L. (2005). Gender discrimination in organizations. In R. L. Dipboye & A. Colella (Eds.), *Discrimination at work: The psychological and organizational bases* (pp. 149–176). New York, NY: Psychology Press.

Cools, S., Markussen, S., & Strøm, M. (2017). Children and careers: How family size affects parents' labor market outcomes in the long run. *Demography, 54*(5), 1773–1793. https://doi.org/10.1007/s13524-017-0612-0

Costa, C., Bakas, F. E., Breda, Z., & Durão, M. (2017). "Emotional" female managers: How gendered roles influence tourism management discourse. *Journal of Hospitality and Tourism Management, 33*, 149–156. http://doi.org/10.1016/j.jhtm.2017.09.011

Costa, C., Bakas, F. E., Breda, Z., Durão, M., Carvalho, I., & Caçador, S. (2017). Gender, flexibility and the "ideal tourism worker." *Annals of Tourism Research, 64*, 64–75. http://doi.org/10.1016/j.annals.2017.03.002

Crosby, F. J., Williams, J. C., & Biernat, M. (2004). The maternal wall. *Journal of Social Issues, 60*, 675–682. https://doi.org/10.1111/j.0022-4537.2004.00379.x

Cuddy, A. J. C., Fiske, S. T., & Glick, P. (2004). When professionals become mothers, warmth doesn't cut the ice. *Journal of Social Issues, 60*(4), 701–718. http://doi. org/10.1111/j.0022-4537.2004.00381.x

Dashper, K. (2019). Mentoring for gender equality: Supporting female leaders in the hospitality industry. *International Journal of Hospitality Management, 88*, 102397. http://doi.org/10.1016/j.ijhm.2019.102397

Davies, A. R., & Frink, B. D. (2014). The origins of the ideal worker: The separation of work and home in the United States from the market revolution to 1950. *Work and Occupations, 41*(1), 18–39.

Deshpande, A. (2020). The COVID-19 pandemic and gendered division of paid and unpaid work: Evidence from India. Paper in Institute for the Study of Labor (IZA), IZA Discussion Paper Series; IZA Discussion Paper No. 13815.

Dezso, C. L., Ross, D. D., & Uribe, J. (2016). Is there an implicit quota on women in top management? A large-sample statistical analysis. *Strategic Management Journal, 37*(1), 98–115.

Doherty, L. (2004). Work–life balance initiatives: Implications for women. *Employee Relations, 26*(4), 433–452. https://doi.org/10.1108/01425450410544524

Eagly, A. H., Johannesen-Schmidt, M. C., & van Engen, M. L. (2003). Transformational, transactional, and laissez-faire leadership styles: A meta-analysis comparing women and men. *Psychological Bulletin, 129*(4), 569–591. https://doi.org/10.1037/0033-2909.129.4.569

Eagly, A. H., & Karau, S. J. (2002). Role congruity theory of prejudice toward female leaders. *Psychological Review, 109*(3), 573–598. https://doi.org/10.1037/0033-295X.109.3.573

Eagly, A. H., Nater, C., Miller, D. I., Kaufmann, M., & Sczesny, S. (2020). Gender stereotypes have changed: A cross-temporal meta-analysis of U.S. public opinion polls from 1946 to 2018. *American Psychologist, 75*(3), 301–315. https://doi.org/10.1037/amp0000494

England, P. (2010). The gender revolution uneven and stalled. *Gender & Society, 24*(2), 149–166.

England, P., Bearak, J., Budig, M. J., & Hodges, M. J. (2016). Do highly paid, highly skilled women experience the largest motherhood penalty? *American Sociological Review, 81*(6), 1161–1189. https://doi.org/10.1177/0003122416673598

Equality Act 2010 (2021, August 25). Retrieved from https://www.legislation.gov.uk/ukpga/2010/15/contents

Exley, C., Niederle, M., & Vesterlund, L. (2016, April). New research: Women who don't negotiate might have a good reason. *Harvard Business Review.* Retrieved from https://hbr.org/2016/04/women-who-dont-negotiate-their-salaries-might-have-a-good-reason

Ferreira Freire Guimarães, C. R., & Silva, J. R. (2016). Pay gap by gender in the tourism industry of Brazil. *Tourism Management, 52*, 440–450. http://doi.org/10.1016/j.tourman.2015.07.003

Fleming, S. S. (2015). Déjà vu? An updated analysis of the gender wage gap in the US hospitality sector. *Cornell Hospitality Quarterly, 56*(2), 180–190. http://dx.doi.org/10.1177/1938965514567680

Galinsky, E., & Matos, K. (2011). The future of work–life fit. *Organizational Dynamics, 40*(4), 267–280.

Ghosh, S., & Bhattacharya, M. (2022). Analyzing the impact of COVID-19 on the financial performance of the hospitality and tourism industries: an ensemble MCDM approach in the Indian context. International Journal of Contemporary Hospitality Management, (ahead-of-print).

Granovetter, M. S. (1973). The strength of weak ties. *American Journal of Sociology, 78*(6), 1360–1380.

Guerrier, Y., & Adib, A. S. (2000). 'No, we don't provide that service': The harassment of hotel employees by customers. *Work, Employment and Society, 14*(4), 689–705. https://doi.org/10.1177/09500170022118680

Heilman, M. E. (2012). Gender stereotypes and workplace bias. *Research in Organizational Behavior, 32*, 113–135. https://doi.org/10.1016/j.riob.2012.11.003

Hicks, L. (1990). Excluded women: How can this happen in the hotel world? *The Service Industries Journal, 10*(2), 348–363. https://doi.org/10.1080/02642069000000035

Hochschild, A. R. (1997). *The time bind: When work becomes home and home becomes work.* New York, NY: Henry Holt Company.

Hoel, H., & Einarsen, S. (2003). *Violence at work in catering, hotels, and tourism.* Geneva: International Labour Office.

Hofstede, G. (2001). *Culture's consequences: Comparing values, behaviors, institutions, and organizations across nations.* Thousand Oaks, CA: Sage Publications.

Huffman, M. L., Cohen, P. N., & Pearlman, J. (2010). Engendering change: Organizational dynamics and workplace gender desegregation, 1975–2005. *Administrative Science Quarterly, 55*(2), 255–277. https://doi.org/10.2189/asqu.2010.55.2.255

International Finance Corporation (IFC). (2017). Women and tourism: Designing for inclusion. Tourism for development knowledge series. Retrieved from https://openknowledge.worldbank.org/handle/10986/28535. Accessed on August 15, 2021.

Jejeebhoy, S. J., Santhya, K. G., Acharya, R., & Prakash, R. (2013). Marriage-related decision-making and young women's marital relations and agency. *Asian Population Studies, 9*(1), 28–49. http://doi.org/10.1080/17441730.2012.736699

Karunarathna, A. (2015). Internal barriers for women career advancement in Sri Lankan hotel industry with special reference to five star hotels in Sri Lanka. *Journal of Scientific and Research Publications, 5*(9), 1–5.

Kattara, H. (2005). Career challenges for female managers in Egyptian hotels. *International Journal of Contemporary Hospitality Management, 17*(3), 238–251. https://doi.org/10.1108/09596110510591927

Kaushal, V., & Srivastava, S. (2020). Hospitality and tourism industry amid COVID-19 pandemic: Perspectives on challenges and learnings from India. *International Journal of Hospitality Management, 92*, 102707. https://doi.org/10.1016/j.ijhm.2020.102707

King, E. B., Botsford, W., Hebl, M. R., Kazama, S., Dawson, J. F., & Perkins, A. (2012). Benevolent sexism at work: Gender differences in the distribution of challenging developmental experiences. *Journal of Management, 38*, 1835–1866. https://doi.org/10.1177/0149206310365902

Koenig, A. M., Eagly, A. H., Mitchell, A. A., & Ristikari, T. (2011). Are leader stereotypes masculine? A meta-analysis of three research paradigms. *Psychological Bulletin, 137*(4), 616–642. https://doi.org/10.1037/a0023557

Korn Ferry Institute. (2017). *When CEOs speak.* Retrieved from https://engage.kornferry.com/Global/FileLib/Women_CEOs_speak/KF-Rockefeller-Women-CEOs-Speak-Nov_2017.pdf. Accessed on June 12, 2021.

Kulkarni, A., & Mishra, M. (2022). Aspects of women's leadership in the organisation: Systematic literature review. *South Asian Journal of Human Resources Management, 9*(1), 9–32. https://doi.org/10.1177/23220937211056139

Kumar, P., & Blake-Beard, S. (2012). What good is bad mentorship? Protégé's perception of negative mentoring experiences. *Indian Journal of Industrial Relations, 48*(1), 79–93. http://www.jstor.org/stable/23509768

Kumar, P., Chakraborty, S., & Kumar, A. (2020). Support system's impact on work-life interface: A study of part-time adult students in India. *Indian Journal of Industrial Relations, 55*(3), 491–505.

Kumar, P., & Singh, G. (2020). *Gender equity in the boardroom: The case of India.* Emerald Group Publishing.

Lauterbach, K. E., & Weiner, B. J. (1996). Dynamics of upward influence. *Leadership Quarterly*, *7*(1), 87–107.

LeanIn.Org & McKinsey & Company. (2016). Women in the workplace. Retrieved from https://wiw-report.s3.amazonaws.com/Women_in_the_Workplace_2016.pdf

LeanIn.Org & McKinsey & Company. (2019). Women in the workplace. Retrieved from https://wiw-report.s3.amazonaws.com/Women_in_the_Workplace_2019.pdf

Leslie, L. M., Manchester, C. F., Park, T., & Mehng, S. A. (2012). Flexible work practices: A source of career premiums or penalties? *Academy of Management Journal*, *55*(6), 1407–1428.

Li, L., & Wang-Leung, R. (2001). Female managers in Asian hotels: Profile and career challenges. *International Journal of Contemporary Hospitality Management*, *13*(4), 189–196. https://doi.org/10.1108/09596110110389511

Lyness, K. S., & Schrader, C. A. (2006). Moving ahead or just moving? An examination of gender differences in senior corporate management appointments. *Group & Organization Management*, *31*, 651–676. https://doi.org/10.1177/1059601106286890

Lyness, K. S., & Thompson, D. E. (2000). Climbing the corporate ladder: Do female and male executives follow the same route? *Journal of Applied Psychology*, *85*, 86–101. https://doi.org/10.1037/0021-9010.85.1.86

Maheshwari, M., & Lenka, U. (2022). Family friendly policies: A double-edged sword? *Industrial and Commercial Training*, *54*(2), 293–316. http://doi.org/10.1108/ICT-05-2021-0034

Manoharan, A., & Singal, M. (2017). A systematic literature review of research on diversity and diversity management in the hospitality literature. *International Journal of Hospitality Management*, *66*, 77–91. https://doi.org/10.1016/j.ijhm.2017.07.002

Marfil Cotilla, M., & Campos-Soria, J. A. (2021). Decomposing the gender wage gap in the hospitality industry: A quantile approach. *International Journal of Hospitality Management*, *94*, 102826. https://doi.org/10.1016/j.ijhm.2020.102826

McKinsey & Company. (2020). Diversity wins. Retrieved from https://www.mckinsey.com/~/media/mckinsey/featured%20insights/diversity%20and%20inclusion/diversity%20wins%20how%20inclusion%20matters/diversity-wins-how-inclusion-matters-vf.pdf?shouldIndex=false. Accessed on August 25, 2021.

McIntosh, B., McQuaid, R., Munro, A., & Dabir-Alai, P. (2012). Motherhood and its impact on career progression. *Gender in Management: An International Journal*, *27*(5), 346–364. https://doi.org/10.1108/17542411211252651

Miles, M. B., & Huberman, A. M. (1994). *Qualitative data analysis: An expanded sourcebook* (2nd ed.). Thousand Oaks, CA: Sage Publications, Inc.

Mohammadi, Z., Bhati, A., & Ng, E. (2022). 20 years of workplace diversity research in hospitality and tourism: A bibliometric analysis. *Equality, Diversity and Inclusion: An International Journal* (ahead-of-print).

Mooney, S., & Ryan, I. (2009). A woman's place in hotel management: Upstairs or downstairs? *Gender in Management: An International Journal*, *24*(3), 195–210. doi:10.1108/17542410910950877

Mooney, S., Ryan, I., & Harris, C. (2017). The intersections of gender with age and ethnicity in hotel careers: Still the same old privileges? *Gender, Work & Organization*, *24*(4), 360–375. https://doi.org/10.1111/gwao.12169

Morgan, N., & Pritchard, A. (2018). Gender matters in hospitality (invited paper for "luminaries" special issue of *International Journal of Hospitality Management*). *International Journal of Hospitality Management*, *76*, 38–44. https://doi.org/10.1016/j.ijhm.2018.06.008

Muñoz-Bullón, F. (2009). The gap between male and female pay in the Spanish tourism industry. *Tourism Management*, *30*(5), 638–649. http://dx.doi.org/10.1016/j.tourman.2008.11.007

Murrell, A. J., & Onosu, G. O. (2022). Mentoring diverse leaders: The necessity of identity work. In R. Ghosh & H. M. Hutchins (Eds.), *HRD perspectives on developmental relationships* (pp. 175–195). Berlin: Springer Books. http://doi.org/10.1007/978-3-030-85033-3_8

Ng, C. W., & Pine, R. (2003). Women and men in hotel management in Hong Kong: Perceptions of gender and career development issues. *International Journal of Hospitality Management, 22*(1), 85–102. https://doi.org/10.1016/s0278-4319(02)00077-4

Oakley, A. (2006). Feminism isn't ready to be swept under the carpet. *The Times Higher Education Supplement*, March 3, pp. 18–19.

Patwardhan, V., Mayya, S., & Joshi, H. G. (2016). Barriers to career advancement of women managers in Indian five star hotels: A gender perspective. *International Journal of Human Resource Studies, 6*(2), 248–271.

Paustian-Underdahl, S. C. (2022). Examining the role of maternity benefit comparisons and pregnancy discrimination in women's turnover decisions. *Personnel Psychology*.

Post, C., & Byron, K. (2015). Women on boards and firm financial performance: A meta-analysis. *Academy of Management Journal, 58*(5), 1546–1571.

Purcell, K. (1996). The relationship between career and job opportunities: Women's employment in the hospitality industry as a microcosm of women's employment. *Women in Management Review, 11*(5), 17–24. http://doi.org/10.1108/09649429610122618

Pylkkänen, E., & Smith, N. (2002). *Career interruptions due to parental leave – A comparative study of Denmark and Sweden.* Economic Studies, Department of Economics, Goteborg University, 120.

Ranjith Kumara, Y. A. D. R. (2018). Career development of women in the hotel industry: An overview. *Journal of Applied and Natural Science, 10*(1), 330–338.

Ravindran, B., & Baral, R. (2014). Factors affecting the work attitudes of Indian re-entry women in the IT sector. *Vikalpa, 39*(2), 31–42. https://doi.org/10.1177/0256090920140205

Reid, E. M., & Ramarajan, L. (2016). Managing the high-intensity workplace. *Harvard Business Review.* Retrieved from https://hbr.org/2016/06/managing-the-high-intensity-workplace

Richard, A. (2021). *Gender invariance of the mediating effect of perceived emotional-social support in the relationship between work–life conflict and occupational stress.* Doctoral dissertation, Stellenbosch University, Stellenbosch.

Risman, B. J. (2004). Gender as a social structure. *Gender & Society, 18*(4), 429–450. http://doi.org/10.1177/0891243204265349

Ryan, M., & Haslam, S. (2005). The glass cliff: Evidence that women are over-represented in precarious leadership positions. *British Journal of Management, 16*, 81–90. https://dx.doi.org/10.1111/j.1467-8551.2005.00433.x

Sanaria, A. D. (2016). A conceptual framework for understanding the impression management strategies used by women in Indian organizations. *South Asian Journal of Human Resources Management, 3*(1), 25–39.

Santos, L. D., & Varejão, J. (2007). Employment, pay and discrimination in the tourism industry. *Tourism Economics, 13*(2), 225–240. https://doi.org/10.5367/000000007780823186

Schein, V. E., & Davidson, M. J. (1993). Think manager, think male. *Management Development Review, 6*(3), 24. https://doi.org/10.1108/EUM0000000000738

Segovia-Pérez, M., Figueroa-Domecq, C., Fuentes-Moraleda, L., & Muñoz-Mazón, A. (2019). Incorporating a gender approach in the hospitality industry: Female executives' perceptions. *International Journal of Hospitality Management, 76*, 184–193.

Sharma, S., & Kaur, R. (2019). Glass ceiling for women and work engagement: The moderating effect of marital status. *FIIB Business Review, 8*(2), 132–146.

Siegel, R., König, C. J., & Zobel, Y. (2020). Executive search consultants' biases against women (or men?). *Frontiers in Psychology, 11*, 541766.

Skalpe, O. (2007). The CEO gender pay gap in the tourism industry—Evidence from Norway. *Tourism Management, 28*(3), 845–853. http://doi.org/10.1016/j.tourman.2006.06.005

Smith, A. E., & Hatmaker, D. M. (2017). Individual stresses and strains in the ascent to leadership: Gender, work, and family. In S. R. Madsen (Ed.), *Handbook of research on gender and leadership* (pp. 304–315). Cheltenham: Edward Elgar Publishing Limited.

S&P Global. (2019). When women lead, firms win. Retrieved from https://www.spglobal.com/_division_assets/images/special-editorial/iif-2019/whenwomenlead_pdf. Accessed on August 24, 2021.

The Castell Project. (2020). Women in hospitality industry leadership 2020. Retrieved from https://www.castellproject.org/. Accessed on May 7, 2021.

The Equal Remuneration Act 1976 (2021, August 25). Retrieved from https://maitri.mahaonline.gov.in/pdf/equal-remuneration-act-1976.pdf#:⬛:text=THE%20EQUAL%20REMUNERATION%20ACT%2C%201976%20%5B25%20OF%201976%5D,and%20for%20matters%20connected%20therewith%20or%20incidental%20thereto

Thrane, C. (2008). Earnings differentiation in the tourism industry: Gender, human capital and socio-demographic effects. *Tourism Management, 29*(3), 514–524. http://doi.org/10.1016/j.tourman.2007.05.017

Tribe, J. (2010). Tribes, territories, and networks in the tourism academy. *Annals of Tourism Research, 37*(1), 7–33.

United Nations Environment Programme, & World Trade Organization (WTO). (2005). *Making tourism more sustainable: A guide for policy makers*. Retrieved from https://wedocs.unep.org/20.500.11822/8741

United Nations World Tourism Organization. (2019). *Global report on women in tourism* (2nd ed.). Retrieved from https://www.unwto.org/publication/global-report-women-tourism-2-edition. Accessed on April 19, 2021.

Van den Brink, M., Brouns, M., & Waslander, S. (2006). Does excellence have a gender? A national research study on recruitment and selection procedures for professorial appointments in The Netherlands. *Employee Relations, 28*(6), 523–539.

Williams, C. L. (1992). The glass escalator: Hidden advantages for men in the "female" professions. *Social Problems, 39*(3), 253–267. http://dx.doi.org/10.1525/sp.1992.39.3.03x0034h

Williams, J. (2000). *Unbending gender: Why family and work conflict and what to do about it.* New York, NY: Oxford University Press.

Williams, J. C. (2004, October). The maternal wall. *Harvard Business Review*. Retrieved from https://hbr.org/2004/10/the-maternal-wall

World Economic Forum (WEF). (2022). The global gender gap report 2022. Retrieved from https://www.weforum.org/reports/global-gender-gap-report-2022/. Accessed on January 15, 2022.

Xiao, J., & Mao, J. Y. (2022). Negative role modeling in hospitality organizations: A social learning perspective of supervisor and subordinate customer-targeted incivility. *International Journal of Hospitality Management, 102*, 103141. https://doi.org/10.1016/j.ijhm.2022.103141

Index

Printed in the USA
CPSIA information can be obtained
at www.ICGtesting.com
JSHW052030080224
56946JS00004B/29